What's Gone Wrong?

What's Gone Wrong?

SOUTH AFRICA ON THE BRINK
OF FAILED STATEHOOD

Alex Boraine

Foreword by
Desmond M Tutu

NEW YORK UNIVERSITY PRESS

Washington Square, New York

First published in the USA in 2014 by
NEW YORK UNIVERSITY PRESS
Washington Square
New York, NY 10003
www.nyupress.org

Originally published in South Africa in 2014 by
JONATHAN BALL PUBLISHERS (PTY) LTD
A division of Media24 Limited
PO Box 33977
Jeppestown
2043

South African spelling and punctuation conventions have been retained.

References to Internet websites (URLs) were accurate at the time of writing.
Neither the author nor New York University Press is responsible for URLs that
may have expired or changed since the manuscript was prepared.

For Library of Congress Cataloging-in-Publication data, please contact the Library of Congress.

ISBN: 978-1-4798-5497-4 (cl)

New York University Press books are printed on acid-free paper,
and their binding materials are chosen for strength and durability.
We strive to use environmentally responsible suppliers and materials
to the greatest extent possible in publishing our books.

Manufactured in the United States of America

10 9 8 7 6 5 4 3 2 1

Also available as an ebook

In memory of Frederik van Zyl Slabbert,
a special friend who never stopped asking questions.

To Jenny, always and forever.

Contents

Acronyms and Abbreviations

ANC   African National Congress
BEE   Black Economic Empowerment
CBO   community-based organisation
CDRA   Community Development Resource Association
Cosatu   Congress of South African Trade Unions
CPSA   Communist Party of South Africa
CSO   civil society organisation
DA   Democratic Alliance
ETT   Electoral Task Team
Idasa   Institute for a Democratic Alternative for South Africa
IEC   Independent Electoral Commission
JSC   Judicial Services Commission
MK   Umkhonto we Sizwe
NDA   National Development Agency
NEC   National Executive Committee (ANC)
NGO   non-governmental organisation
NLB   National Lottery Board
NLDTF   National Lottery Distribution Trust Fund
NPO   nonprofit organisation
NUM   National Union of Mineworkers
NWC   National Working Committee (ANC)
OAU   Organisation of African Unity
PAC   Pan Africanist Congress
R2K   Right2Know
REAP   Rural Education Access Programme
SACP   South African Communist Party
Sadtu   South African Democratic Teachers Union

SANDF	South African National Defence Force
SASO	South African Students Organisation
SCAT	Social Change Assistance Trust
Scopa	Standing Committee on Public Accounts
SIU	Special Investigating Unit
TAC	Treatment Action Campaign
TRC	Truth and Reconciliation Commission
UDF	United Democratic Front
UDM	United Democratic Movement
UN	United Nations

Foreword by Desmond M Tutu, Archbishop Emeritus

Chatting recently with someone very close to a top ANC leader, I remarked: 'We are where we were with the apartheid nationalists. They didn't ask what qualifications you had for a particular job. No, they asked, "What is your political affiliation?"'

I was startled at first when she exclaimed: 'No!' But then she went on to say, 'It is worse: they ask which faction of the ruling party you support.'

We are in dire straits in our beloved country. In this hard-hitting volume, Alex Boraine incisively and with great perspicacity answers the question so many are asking: 'What's gone wrong?' Why, instead of working to eradicate poverty, do we have the widest gap between rich and poor globally; why do the nouveaux riches flaunt their often ill-gotten wealth so much, existing cheek by jowl with demeaning squalor? Much of our public service is in a dismal state. Our public hospitals and schools in the 'black' townships leave a great deal to be desired. We have high levels of unemployment and violent crime. Corruption, frequently brazen, seems to be the order of the day. Effective law enforcement agencies are disbanded. A competent and principled national director of prosecutions was shown the door because he wanted to charge the then commissioner of police and Jacob Zuma, then deputy president. The government has treated with utter disdain a High Court order to produce the secret tapes whose contents were the grounds for dropping charges against Mr Zuma before he became president. It is odd that they should be so bashful about revealing evidence that those charges against him were contaminated by a political conspiracy.

We applaud the government for providing free education for many children. But it is an awful indictment that there are children learning under trees in this day and age. Recently, learners in one province were seriously handicapped by non-delivery of required textbooks. These were later discovered piled high in a rubbish dump. No one was held accountable for this disgraceful faux pas. In a healthy democracy, the government minister responsible would have taken political responsibility and resigned.

The president flouted common practice when he passed over a widely respected deputy chief justice and appointed someone else. The deputy chief justice had declared at his birthday party that his loyalty was not to any political party but to the Constitution. Most people would have said he was stating the obvious. In our South Africa, the ruling party took umbrage. And thereby hangs a tale.

Boraine has impeccable credentials for the task he has set himself. He is the youngest person ever to be elected president of the Methodist Church of SA Conference. He did resign on principle from a whites-only apartheid parliament when it became clear it was really a charade where the nationalists could do anything because of their massive majority. He began to concentrate on transitional justice – that is, what happens when a country makes the transition from an oppressive unrepresentative dispensation to democracy, what has to happen to make perpetrators accountable, how do you heal the trauma of the victims; and he became founding president of the highly regarded International Centre for Transitional Justice with headquarters in New York. He was a most effective deputy chairperson of our Truth and Reconciliation Commission, then a visiting law professor at New York University. And he loves South Africa passionately. He could have lived in New York forever. But he and Jenny, his wife, love their motherland passionately.

Alex was a member of delegations that met with the ANC in exile. He suggests that it was in the 30 years of exile that the trouble started. The ANC in exile was concerned with seizure of power. From the nature of things, decisions had to be taken without too much discussion in order to frustrate infiltrators who were thick on the ground. The internal anti-apartheid opposition, on the other hand, insisted on thorough discussions, with decisions most often being taken by consensus. When Allan Boesak and I announced the Peace March of September 1989, I was asked: 'Where did you get your mandate?' I shut them up when I replied, 'From God!'

For the ANC members, their ultimate loyalty is not to the country or the state. No, their loyalty is to the party. The party is über alles. Thus it is not for them odd or illegal to recall a serving president of the country. He is, ultimately, just another member, just another cadre. It is not at all surprising that President Zuma can give vent to his frustration when the Constitutional Court rules that some government action or draft legislation is unconstitutional, and declare unequivocally that the ANC have the majority and cannot tolerate being frustrated by some pesky Constitutional Court. Thus speaks a majoritarian, not a true democrat who took an oath to uphold the Constitution at all times as the ultimate authority in the land. It is thus not surprising when what are declared to be state occasions are turned into ANC rallies. At both the memorial service and the state funeral for former President Nelson Mandela, none of the other South African political parties featured at all.

Mercifully, we South Africans are made of nobler stuff. We showed it when we listened to Madiba's call to walk the path of forgiveness and reconciliation instead of revenge and retribution when we made the transition from injustice and oppression to freedom and democracy. We have the human and natural resources to become a scintillating success instead of a failed state and Boraine shows some of what we need to do in his chapters on civil society, parliament and, especially, realignment in politics.

This is a most worthwhile, indeed invigorating, read!

January 2014

Introduction

On 24 April 1994, I was approached by a delegation from my neighbours. I was stunned by their request. They asked if they could stay in our home on Election Day. They expressed their fear and concern that the election was going to be very violent. But more to the point, they were afraid that black voters would attack white homes: 'They will do to us what we have been doing to them for years.' They told me that they had stored canned goods and water on the slopes of Table Mountain in case shops were burned down. These were professional people who saw only a dangerous future should the ANC win the election.

I assured them that the ANC was not seeking revenge. Nevertheless, I could understand some of their apprehension. Like so many whites, they were hopelessly out of touch and did not accept Mandela's repeated assurances that the election would be peaceful. After all, wide-scale violence had taken place throughout the negotiations and even as we spoke blood was running in the streets of Johannesburg and Germiston. The right wing was determined that there would be no peaceful election. Despite this, I told them they would be safe in their homes, and I urged them to cast their votes on 27 April.

I am not sure what happened to the canned goods and water stored on the mountainside; hopefully they were snapped up by the homeless!

Many years later, in 2012, I was with a group of friends talking about books. When we broke for a glass of wine, they began very forcibly to express their disappointment and disquiet at the current state of politics in South Africa. According to them, there was something rotten, not in the state of Denmark, but very much closer to home. Several referred to the incidence of attempted bribery by traffic police and by officials in the car licensing department. Others complained of corruption on a massive scale in the public service, in local government and even in the leadership of the ANC. 'The courts are in a shambles, dockets are conveniently lost, witnesses are threatened and money changes hands,' they protested. Another mentioned the inefficiencies in government departments because of the deployment of inexperienced persons, particularly at local government level.

As I listened to them spilling out a litany of woes, I wondered if Alan Paton's cry had come back to haunt us. What has gone wrong in the beloved country?

After all, South Africa had experienced highly successful negotiations after years of oppression and resistance. Despite the attendant violence, we won through and the birth of a new South Africa was celebrated with a brilliant Interim Constitution which emerged from the discussions and was consolidated two years later; the first democratic election in our history was a resounding success. Who will ever forget the laughing and the tears as millions of voters voted for the very first time. Amongst those who voted for the first time in their lives were Nelson Mandela and Archbishop Desmond Tutu.

Once the polecat of the world, we had become the darling of the international community. We had suffered a period of isolation because of apartheid policies, but this was now behind us. People of all races rejoiced that we could now participate in the Olympic Games and in international sports, music and drama.

At first, things went so smoothly. Racist laws were repealed; schools, colleges and universities were open to all races; cinemas, parks, housing, likewise. There was a mood of relief, of confidence. Millions gained access to clean water; many township residents who used to read by candlelight now had access to electricity; there was free access to hospitals for the sick and grant-in-aid for the very poor. Our economy grew, and peace broke out throughout the land. Above all, we had in Nelson Mandela a leader of world-class proportions. He was essentially Mr Reconciler, winning the admiration of even the fiercest opponents of the ANC. He was the quintessence of humanity. He embraced former enemies, visited synagogues, mosques and churches, while remaining true to his own secular beliefs. He seemed to love all humanity and we loved him in return. So what went wrong?

* * *

Mandela's presidency was essentially the honeymoon period in the new dispensation. The negotiations had succeeded – but they were negotiations conducted by the elite. What of the past horrors of apartheid and its many thousands of victims? Mandela strongly supported the Truth and Reconciliation Commission, which was a time of truth-telling, of healing and a challenge to those in the apartheid government who were in denial. I have written at length about the genesis and proceedings of the TRC,[1] but it can never be over-emphasised how different things would have been if its scores of recommendations – including an urgent and strong plea for economic justice and equality for all South Africans – had been followed.

The commission received consistent and warm support from Mandela, even when it came under severe attack from the then National Party and its leader, former president FW de Klerk. Ironically, he also had to defend the Final Report of the commission against his deputy president, Thabo Mbeki, who tried unsuccessfully to prevent its publication because he believed there was not sufficient distinction between the violence of the state and the human rights violations committed by the liberation forces. In this regard he was dead wrong. The commission could not be any clearer than it is when it states in its report,

> Any analysis of human rights violations which occurred during the conflicts of the past and any attempt to prevent a recurrence of such violations must take cognisance of the fact that at the heart of the conflict stood an illegal, oppressive and inhuman system imposed on the majority of South Africans without their consent.[2]

Despite Mandela's full support I think the majority of the cabinet followed Mbeki's line and thus the recommendations made by the commission were not given the priority they deserved. It was the justice department's responsibility to follow up on the report but because the report covered a wide range of departments we suggested to government that it should appoint a joint committee which would include Finance, Justice, Health, Housing and Social Welfare. This was never done. The new government, it is true, had many calls on its time and treasury in the early years of rule, but it is shameful that it took so long to respond and when it did, responded so inadequately. The pleas of Desmond Tutu and myself by letter, by e-mail, by public statements, fell on deaf ears.

It is difficult to quantify how the government's intransigence affected the life and work of the TRC. Suffice to say the victims were disillusioned and the momentum towards healing of the nation and reconciliation was lost. With over R1 billion still lying unused in the President's Fund – intended in terms of the TRC Act to compensate apartheid victims – President Mbeki's stalling of the process appears to have blighted the commitment of the department of justice to distribute the money. Failure of political will, it would seem.

*　*　*

After an outstanding period as president, Mandela kept his promise to serve only one term. Thabo Mbeki was elected president in his stead, although Mandela's choice was Cyril Ramaphosa, who had played such a key role in the negotiations – Mbeki was the ANC's chosen successor, trained for the job over years in exile in which he was totally immersed in the party. Mbeki was essentially Mr Manager, a trained economist who focused on sound economic principles. This enabled his administration to provide clean water for millions of poverty-stricken South Africans, to build houses and clinics and schools. The treasury made sufficient money available, but Mbeki started the rot of deploying people into jobs for which they had no experience; as a result service delivery never matched the needs of the poorest of the poor.

Much has been made of the major mistakes and bad judgement we witnessed during Mbeki's presidency. In particular, he will never be allowed to forget, nor will South Africa, his stance on HIV/Aids. It is no exaggeration to claim that thousands of lives would have been spared if he and his government had come to their senses earlier.

Despite Mark Gevisser's brilliant and exhaustive biography, Mbeki remains, for me at least, an enigma. I cannot comprehend his remoteness, the bad calls, his lack of wisdom and judgement in so many different ways. Even less can I grasp his coldness and aloofness. This was not the Mbeki that some of us knew well before 1994.

According to Gevisser, Mbeki argued that as long as he talked about reconciliation whites were happy. However, when he argued for transformation, those same whites were upset and accused him of playing them for useful idiots.[3] This is sheer nonsense. Those of us who were with Mbeki in Dakar acknowledged then the absolute necessity for transformation, and in the TRC recommendations, the commission declared that without economic justice reconciliation would wither on the vine.

Mbeki's downfall came not so much because of his favouritism, his lengthy absences from South Africa, his coldness, his authoritarianism, but because of his sacking of Jacob Zuma as deputy president. In strictly legal and moral terms it was the right decision, but, seen as a way of dealing with someone who was a strong political rival, it also apparently broke a deeply rooted tenet of ANC culture – never set yourself above the party. This action united forces within the ANC who resented Mbeki's dictatorial approach – a useful glimpse, perhaps, into the kind of forces that may some day dislodge Zuma.

Mbeki was resoundingly beaten in the election for president of the ANC at Polokwane, which set off a bitter personal attack and, a few months later, his recall as president of South Africa. This action by the national executive of the ANC was unconstitutional. Mbeki was elected by parliament and only parliament could fire him. But the party trumped parliament and Mbeki accepted his fate, possibly because of his commitment to the ANC – or to secure his pension and status as ex-president. If he had not accepted the action by his own party, it would have unleashed consequences which could have threatened the stability of the country, so perhaps he was wise in bowing to the pressure to resign. Whatever else is true, it demonstrated a spirit of revenge in the ANC, and its contempt for parliament; the party had supreme authority.

* * *

Jacob Zuma became president not only of the ANC but also of South Africa, despite a sordid rape trial (at the end of which he was found not guilty) and charges of corruption which were withdrawn but may yet come back to haunt him. Thus far he has shown remarkable agility in avoiding the consequences of his alleged actions, assisted by the disarray in law enforcement procedures and his friends in court who are hell-bent on protecting him.

Ever since Zuma's election to the highest office in the land things have gone badly wrong. Wherever we look – education, health, safety and security, unemployment, lack of housing and basic facilities, police brutality, inefficiency, mismanagement, jobs for pals, the right of entitlement of the ruling party, corruption in the public service and at every level of government – we see signs of a failing state. The greed and maladministration displayed by government officials can only be described as obscene. Terence Nombembe, the outgoing Auditor-General, stated recently that public officials at local, provincial and national level simply ignore adverse audit reports, and repeat offenders are the order of the day.

A culture of impunity has set in and has become entrenched in the public service over the past five years. The ANC leadership either denies the gravity of the situation or ignores the warning signals. Even when they do acknowledge malpractices and corruption, it is as if they are talking about someone else, and they take no responsibility for ongoing failures. Certainly action very rarely follows even these observations. It is tempting to come to the conclusion that the leadership is part and parcel of the problem and is therefore unable or unwilling to act against the culprits.

Zuma and his team have persisted in their policy of redeployment of party faithful, including those who fail in a given position, which appears to be based not on merit but on loyalty to the party – so once again the party comes above all else. It is hardly surprising therefore to see the decay in so many areas of government.

Coupled with corruption and inefficiency, there is a growing climate of intolerance within the ANC. Its statements often show hostility to any criticism, whether from opposition parties, civil society or the media. Despite assurances of its commitment to constitutional democracy, there are signs that the ANC is growing impatient with some of the decisions taken by the Constitutional Court – and some of its leaders, including the minister of justice and Zuma himself, hint very strongly that the Constitution may have to be amended. A view often expressed is, 'We won the election and we should be able to determine our own political programme without interference from the Constitutional Court.'

Under ANC rule parliament has become in the minds of many a virtual lame duck. I will return to this in more detail in a later chapter. Suffice it to say that there are numerous incidents which indicate the ANC's contempt for the parliamentary process.

It has become increasingly difficult to determine who is governing South Africa. Is it the executive (the president and his cabinet) or Luthuli House (the ANC secretary-general and his staff)? The government or the party? What is the role of the tripartite alliance? How strong is the influence of the South African Communist Party and/or Cosatu? The meetings of the tripartite alliance are held in secret, so it is not possible to assess who has the last word.

While the ANC can rightfully claim that it has made progress in providing services such as housing, clean water, electricity, infrastructure, and so on, there are still many towns and villages and schools which lack basic services. This, together with poor management and often corrupt leadership at local level, has led to an increase in delivery protests. Hardly a day goes by when protests and demonstrations do not take place somewhere in South Africa. Strike action has increased – and what is more worrying is that both delivery protests and strike action are almost always accompanied by violence. Property is destroyed, shops are looted, crops are burned and often someone is injured or even killed.

* * *

What has gone wrong? This is the question on many people's lips. What accounts for the general unease, the lack of confidence, the growing criticism from within and without the party? What accounts for the disillusionment amongst a growing number of the very poor who were promised 'a better life for all'? Is it as simple as party chauvinism, poor leadership, a climate of entitlement by the ruling party, jettisoning of moral compass, bad judgement, incompetence? Certainly responsibility must be laid at the door of successive administrations under the presidencies of Mbeki and Zuma. But is that a good enough answer to the question of how South Africa has slipped so far from the early months and years of apparent unity and prosperity?

Could it be that it all started way back, before the negotiations in 1990? The ANC was in exile for 30 years. During that period the conditions under which its people lived and worked, and the challenges they faced, cultivated a certain climate which was not abandoned on their return to South Africa in 1990. Plagued as the ANC was with informers and differences of opinions regarding strategy, loyalty to the party was paramount. Even in the 1980s, when it became a government-in-waiting, the only government it knew was the party. Is this slavish allegiance to the party which threatens to take South Africa down the road to a one-party state a possible explanation for the dysfunctionality of present-day South Africa? Can we go further and inquire whether 'seizure of power', the popular slogan during the period of exile, is still the aim of at least some of the key leaders in the ANC and possibly in the SACP and Cosatu?

In order to answer this question we need to interrogate the ANC in exile, how it sought to survive the conditions which prevailed then and to meet the challenges which beset it at every turn. What did 'seizure of power' mean then – and is this still the aim of the current ANC leadership?

CHAPTER ONE

The ANC in Exile: Early Years

There continued to be broad agreement on the ultimate objective, the seizure of power, and the necessity for armed struggle or military action to achieve this.
— THOMAS KARIS AND GAIL GERHART, *FROM PROTEST TO CHALLENGE*[1]

Forty-eight years after its founding, the African National Congress was banned in terms of the Unlawful Organisations Act of 1960. Its voice was effectively silenced but its determination to resist the harsh and all-pervading racial policies of the state hardened.

Since its inception in 1912 the ANC had campaigned for participation in the political system in South Africa, from which blacks had been excluded by a deal struck between the Boers and the British after the Anglo-Boer War.

For decades the ANC opposition to successive white governments was hardly revolutionary. Letters were written, delegations sought audiences here and in the UK, all to no avail. Whites were determined to hold on to power at all costs. Despite growing desperation and occasional work stoppages, nothing broke the deadlock of a white minority using increasingly tough legislation and a growing security force on the one hand and an increasingly impatient black majority on the other. It was the politics of oppression and exclusivity versus the politics of resistance. But it should be stressed that the resistance was largely benign.

There was a lull in the strong opposition by the ANC to the white government in the 1930s and 1940s, but the Communist Party of South Africa was growing in strength and many of its members were urged to join the ANC because of the fear of the CPSA being banned (which it was in 1950, under the Suppression of Communism Act).

In the meantime, the 1948 election which brought the National Party to power was a critical step in the shift towards the armed struggle. ANC president Albert Luthuli spoke of his frustration:

> Who will deny that thirty years of my life have been spent knocking in vain, patiently, moderately and modestly at a closed and barred door? Has there been any reciprocal tolerance or moderation from the Government, be it Nationalist or United Party? No! On the contrary, the past thirty years have seen the greatest number of laws restricting our rights and progress until today we have reached a stage where we have almost no rights at all. It is with this background and with a full sense of responsibility that, under the auspices of the African National Congress, I have joined my people in the new spirit that revolts openly and boldly against injustice and expresses itself in a determined and nonviolent manner ...[2]

April 1952 saw the beginning of the Defiance Campaign of peaceful protest against unjust laws and in 1955 the Freedom Charter was launched as the statement of the core principles of the South African Congress Alliance, which consisted of the African National Congress and its allies – the South African Indian Congress, the South African Congress of Democrats and the Coloured People's Congress. Its opening statement was: 'The People Shall Govern!' But these actions only prompted the state to go onto the offensive and in 1956, 156 members of the Congress Alliance were indicted on charges of treason.

This was a huge tactical error on the part of the state. For years a group of anti-apartheid activists from all parts of South Africa were given the opportunity to sit together, to share views and plan strategy – and to be won over by the eloquence of ANC leaders like Mandela and Sisulu. In the end the charges were dismissed and the activists were free to return to their homes to continue their opposition to apartheid with renewed vigour.

For several years there were heated discussions on the need to change strategies and to become more militant, but it was in only in the 1960s that the debate became more charged. On 21 March 1960, police opened fire on a peaceful protest against the pass laws organised by the Pan Africanist Congress (PAC). Sixty-nine people died and this sparked off violent protests in many parts of the country. The tragic events in Sharpeville strongly influenced the abandonment of passive resistance. The government responded by declaring a state of emergency and banning the ANC and PAC. Mandela and the rest of the ANC leadership were forced to go underground.

In December 1961 the momentous decision was taken to shift towards a military solution. No one could have imagined that this would be the start of 30 years of struggle at home and abroad. It was a contentious decision; certainly Chief Albert Luthuli was opposed to the idea and continued to favour passive resistance. But there was a strong man in the person of Nelson Mandela who declared that enough was enough. He saw no alternative to the armed struggle to gain freedom and justice for the oppressed masses. This saw the birth of Umkhonto we Sizwe (MK).

If Mandela was central to the decision, so too was the SACP, as the Communist Party was known from its re-establishment in 1953; he was strongly influenced by their view that the time had come to shift towards an armed struggle. In a sense, it was the SACP that led the way to this new strategy. Its pressure helped to sway an uncertain ANC to opt for violence in response to the violence of the state.

Direct relations between the Communist Party of the Soviet Union and the underground SACP had been established in 1960, and in following years the Soviet Union took up the anti-apartheid cause in the United Nations General Assembly – which the National Party government took as confirmation that South Africa was at the centre of the USSR's plans for communist world domination.[3] The National Democratic Revolution – the Stalin-era Soviet theory on national liberation movements – is still part of ANC policy now.

* * *

The arrest of Mandela and the rest of the ANC leadership remaining in South Africa is history, as is the Rivonia trial of 1963. In a moving speech at a conference sponsored by the World Council of Churches in Kitwe (then Northern Rhodesia) in May 1964, a senior and much-loved ANC member, ZK Matthews, outlined the reasons why the ANC had decided to turn to the armed struggle:[4]

> For many years the Africans reluctantly accepted the rule of the white man but endeavoured to fight for the amelioration of their lot and the removal of the disabilities under which they labour by the usual methods of persuasion and discussion. …[but] non-white groups are faced with a white population which is apparently impervious to the democratic processes of persuasion and discussion.

Matthews quotes from one of Mandela's famous speeches:

> At the beginning of 1961 … I and some colleagues came to the conclusion that as violence in this country was inevitable, it would be unrealistic and wrong for African leaders to continue preaching peace and non-violence when the government met our peaceful demands with force. Umkhonto was to perform sabotage and strict instructions were given to its members right from the start that on no account were they to injure or kill people in planning or carrying out operations.

Matthews concluded his speech with a question:

> When the flower of African youth represented by men such as Mandela or Dr Alexander are being sentenced to long terms of imprisonment during peace time, for fighting for their legitimate rights in what they believe to be the only ways open to them, can we say that the Christian thing is to advise them to acquiesce in their present situation and wait, Micawber-like, for something to turn up?

It had been decided in 1960 to send Oliver Tambo out of the country to head up the ANC's external mission. His mandate was to keep the movement alive and to be the voice of the ANC in Africa and the wider world. Tambo was a quiet, almost diffident person, noted for his belief in the importance of consensus, but often criticised for not being strong enough and not acting more swiftly in times of dissension and division within the ranks of the ANC. He battled to gain the support of those who joined him in exile.

Tambo served as acting president of the movement for many years and was only elected president in 1977. As a committed Christian and someone who had wanted to be an Anglican priest, there must have been considerable inner tension for the ANC leader. I confess that I was surprised when I dined with him for the first time in Lusaka and he said grace before the meal. However, despite his quiet demeanour he played a dominant role in holding a disparate group of people together for some 30 years. He was an excellent diplomat and managed to persuade many leaders in the East and later in the West of the rightness of the ANC's cause.

In my view at least, Tambo has never received adequate acknowledgement for the role he played while the ANC was in exile. It was a tragedy that he suffered a stroke when victory was in sight and never lived to see his beloved party come to power in 1994.

If the movement in exile was struggling for survival against impossible odds, within South Africa throughout the 1960s the ANC was virtually moribund. The banning order in 1960 was serious enough, but the life sentences of Mandela, Walter Sisulu, Govan Mbeki and others were a body blow to the movement. Here and there small groups tried valiantly to keep the ANC visible but the Nationalist security forces cracked down relentlessly and any suggestion of opposition was swiftly squashed.

* * *

It is difficult to comprehend from a distance just how problematic exile was for the ANC during the first 10 years. They started with nothing but their wits and their determination to keep the movement alive. They watched with horror as events unfolded in South Africa and realised there was no point in looking for support from their comrades who faced imprisonment and harassment at every turn. They were on their own. Communication was difficult and dangerous.

The challenges facing Tambo and his compatriots were formidable. They were in a foreign land, money was tight, support from the African continent was lukewarm and housing was often temporary and inade-quate. They were parted from families and friends, and loneliness was a daily companion. It is no wonder that in those first months and years there was considerable frustration and disillusionment. The movement from very early on seemed to be riddled with informers and this not only put it at risk but made it difficult to develop trust; instead suspicion became a hallmark. Some of the informers were former ANC cadres who were turned after torture by the security forces. The ANC became aware of this strategy at great cost to themselves and their paranoia concerning the in-filtration of informers was understandable and almost excusable.

Professor Tom Lodge makes the valid point that 'the terrain of exile is not wholly disadvantageous for the development of a political movement. It can provide protection, security, powerful forms of external support, factors and conditions which facilitate the development of a form and quality of organisation unattainable in the precarious circumstances of opposition parties within the homeland.'5 However, he acknowledges that the first decade was precarious and that a resurgence only took place after the Soweto uprising in 1976.

Fortunately for the ANC, the Communist Party was in far better shape. A number of its leaders – Joe Slovo, Yusuf Dadoo, Moses Kotane, and others – had gone into exile earlier. They were better organised, they had access to guns and money and had a well-developed strategy. They in-troduced the ANC leadership to the current government of the Soviet Union. Many ANC members went to the Soviet Union and East Germany for military training and the Soviets were their biggest supplier of arms and ammunition as well as financial support.

The slogan adopted very early on by the ANC in exile, and used consist-ently throughout this period, was 'seizure of power', but in many respects it was powerless and rhetoric trumped successful action. It was to the cred-it of Tambo and his lieutenants that the ANC existed at all in the first 10 years in exile. However, despite their efforts to hold the movement together there were deep divisions which came close to destroying it. Many of the cadres lived in squalid conditions and wanted nothing more than to return to South Africa and continue the fight against the regime. It was, however, proving very difficult for MK to gain any momentum, largely because of the strength of the South African security forces, the inexperience of the ANC military leaders and the large numbers of informers.

There was tremendous pressure on the ANC to prove that it was capable of leading the fight against apartheid, and this led to a decision to link up with the Zimbabwean liberation movement for an incursion across Rhodesia to establish a route into South Africa. The abortive Wankie mission resulted in great loss of life. But the pressure from dissatisfied cadres brought about the ANC's first national consultative conference – the Morogoro Conference – in Tanzania in 1969.

For some time there had been a keenly felt frustration amongst the rank and file, who previously had not been consulted on policy matters as regards the lack of leadership or strategy to offer any genuine opposition to the apartheid regime. Wankie veteran Chris Hani was particularly critical, especially of the high life of the leadership – including the likes of Thabo Mbeki studying comfortably in Sussex while Hani and his comrades were risking death or imprisonment – and his Memorandum summing up the grievances of those living in camps was a flashpoint which found considerable support amongst his colleagues.

Hani was especially severe in his criticism of the MK military leadership following the abortive raid in Wankie, noting that 'there had never been an attempt to send the leadership inside the country since the Rivonia arrests' and that there was 'an overconcentration of people in offices'. He also railed at 'the careerism of the ANC leadership abroad who have, in every sense, become professional politicians', at 'the opening of mysterious business enterprises' often run by 'dubious characters with shady political backgrounds', and 'the glaring practice of nepotism where the leadership uses its positions to promote their kith and kin and put them in positions where they will not be any physical confrontation with the enemy'.[6]

Although Hani went on to be one of the best-loved members of the ANC, the leadership's first reaction was to see the Memorandum as open rebellion. He and his seven co-signatories were suspended, and if a military tribunal had had its way, would have faced a firing squad.[7]

Despite the lack of an immediate response to the serious grievances and frustrations raised by the 70 delegates, Morogoro was in many ways a turning point. It was a consultative conference which enabled delegates to express their frustration and dissatisfaction with the leadership, the lack of communication and the lack of real progress in the struggle.

The conference also had to give attention to a serious setback, namely the Lusaka Manifesto, which had been adopted on 16 April 1969 by 14 African heads of state and was endorsed by the Organisation of African Unity (OAU) and the General Assembly of the United Nations. At its heart was a call for the ANC to work towards a negotiated settlement to end apartheid. This was a disheartening and severe blow to the ANC, which had less than 10 years earlier resolved that it had no alternative but to turn to the armed struggle because of the intransigence of the South African state. The Manifesto starkly demonstrated the continent's lack of faith in the ANC's ability to bring about the desired transformation. Perhaps this was the first planting of the seeds which finally led the ANC to accept that negotiating with the South African government was the only way to achieve its aims.

The ANC wisely made no attempt to criticise the Manifesto but it certainly concentrated the mind and made it easier to endorse the document entitled 'Strategy and Tactics', which was largely the work of Joe Slovo, MK chief of staff and SACP central committee member, and illustrated yet again the influence of the Communist Party on the ANC.[8] Essentially, Slovo's document stressed the need to hold political work in tension with the use of military force: 'The primacy of the political leadership is unchallenged and supreme and all revolutionary formations and levels (whether armed or not) are subordinate to this leadership.'[9] Therefore political mobilisation was of paramount importance. Despite his strong assertion the ANC in exile remained ambivalent about the primacy of political mobilisation over the armed struggle.

There were other important decisions taken: a streamlined executive was elected (from 23 down to 9 members), Tambo was re-elected as acting president by acclamation and ANC membership was opened to all irrespective of race, although the executive remained exclusively African. Further, a Revolutionary Council was appointed to give effect to what Slovo had proposed, namely, the holding together of the political and the military. It was headed by Tambo with Yusuf Dadoo as vice-chairman and included Slovo and Reginald September, making the membership completely non-racial.

Despite the fact that the conference did not solve the acute organisational and strategic weaknesses which beset the movement, it certainly
gave a jump start into the 1970s, which saw the beginning of a much more
cohesive and effective movement. In his closing remarks, Oliver Tambo
warned delegates to –

> … wage a relentless war against disrupters and defend the ANC against
> provocateurs and enemy agents. Defend the revolution against enemy
> propaganda, whatever form it takes. Be vigilant comrades. The enemy
> is vigilant. Beware of the wedge-driver, the man who creeps from ear
> to ear, carrying a bag full of wedges, driving them in between you and
> the next man, between a group and another, a man who goes round
> creating splits and divisions. Beware of the wedge-driver, comrades.
> Watch his poisonous tongue.[10]

*   *   *

Two major events in South Africa in the 1970s influenced and challenged
the ANC in exile. The first was the birth of the Black Consciousness
Movement under the inspiring leadership of Steve Biko. The impact this
movement had on young people in particular cannot be underestimated
and we will never know how extensive and deep its influence would have
been had Biko not been killed by the security forces on 12 September 1977.
While it had no programme of action, its philosophy encouraged self-
worth and black pride amongst thousands of young people. It revived the
spirit which had been largely crushed by the powerful state. The founding
of the South African Students Organisation (SASO) soon attracted young
blacks, at first from universities and colleges but later also from schools. In
July 1971 Black Consciousness was defined in the SASO Policy Manifesto:
'Black Consciousness is an attitude of mind, a way of life. The basic tenet
of black consciousness is that the black man must reject all value systems
that seek to make him a foreigner in the country of his birth and reduce
his basic dignity. The black man must build up his own value systems, see
himself as self-defined and not as defined by others.'

17

Biko had a remarkable ability to express himself clearly and powerfully. He inspired all who listened to him encouraging blacks to stand tall, to be proud and to refuse to bow down to the white man. But he was no racist. I recall a discussion we had on my stoop in Durban. Biko was a member of the Student Christian Movement at Wentworth Medical School and together we often addressed conferences of young people. We met several times in my home. On this particular occasion he told me that this would be his last visit. I was puzzled but he explained, 'We must separate so that we can come together under different circumstances. White and black are unequal under apartheid. We as blacks must go it alone, must assert our own human dignity; only then can we come together as equals to discuss the new South Africa.' Nevertheless, Biko and I kept in touch until his arrest and death in detention:

> When I was in Parliament and he was banned in King William's Town we often corresponded and talked on the telephone. Ironically, I used the Parliamentary letterhead knowing full well that it would be opened and read by the Security Police. One day he called, highly agitated, to tell me that his lover Mamphela Ramphele had been arrested and detained. He asked me to make it widely known, and to talk to the minister of police. I talked with Louis le Grange but to no avail.
>
> The last time I saw Steve was after he had been banished to the King William's Town area, where he was born. I went to see him and we walked in the fields, because the buildings were obviously bugged. We talked about many things. He was extraordinarily eloquent; his eyes shone with his commitment. When we parted he said: 'You and I are in very different places. You are in Parliament with the Progressive Party, and I am here working, banned, but I would welcome an opportunity for you and your party and me and my group to come together to discuss what our scenario is for a new South Africa. What would it mean in concrete terms?' I said I was quite sure there were many of us who would welcome such a discussion and undertook to talk to Colin Eglin. I did, and Colin later travelled to see Steve.
>
> As I turned to leave that day, I said: 'Steve, for God's sake be careful; they hate you and they are going to get you if you break your banning

order. Please, please be safe.' He smiled and waved and turned away. I think he really believed that he was almost invincible.[11]

The rise of Black Consciousness and its impact on young blacks must have come as a surprise and a shock to the ANC in exile. While they would support the call for blacks to assert themselves and to throw off the inferiority imposed by white supremacists who supported laws which placed blacks in an inferior position in every walk of life, it was not on the initiative of the ANC that this movement came about. Indeed, Biko was critical of both the ANC and the Pan Africanist Congress. Certainly, the young people he influenced had hardly heard of the ANC. The ANC in exile was concerned that SASO and related bodies would rival its claim to be the chief representative of all blacks in South Africa.

The second major event within South Africa came as an even greater shock to the ANC. This was the 1976 Soweto uprising. To be fair, it took most people by surprise, including the apartheid government. This despite the warnings issued by the Progressive Federal Party in parliament. Bantu education was anathema to blacks and the decision to impose Afrikaans as a language medium of instruction in black schools was the last straw for children who had experienced inferior education all their young lives. (I was physically threatened by a National Party member who blamed my party for the slaughter which took place on that fateful day, 16 June 1976. Albert Notnagel confronted me in the dining room of parliament, quivering with rage, and looked set to strike me. I left him with his mouth open and red with anger. Once again, the messenger is blamed.)

Behind the resentment and the determination to protest was the influence of Black Consciousness, which not only impacted on university students but also on school children who attended formation sessions conducted by SASO. In these formation classes young people were politicised and encouraged to reject the overcrowding in classrooms, the lack of facilities and the general second-rate education offered to blacks compared to that offered to whites. This was a new generation in strong contrast to the passivity of their elders. Older black leaders watched helplessly as brave and angry teenagers, and even younger children, confronted the police. They watched as their children went on the rampage, destroying every possible institutional symbol of apartheid. They watched as their children were shot and killed by the police. Gutter education was unacceptable.

The uprising spread like wildfire, not only in nearby Witwatersrand townships but in many parts of South Africa. The police were both inept and ruthless, the government at a loss as to how to restore order. Whites were deeply shocked and began to realise that blacks were not 'a happy, smiling lot'. All in all, it was a sea change in South African politics and a precursor of greater militancy to come. But in the end, the security forces were too strong: the protests were ruthlessly put down and families counted the dead.

The Soweto uprising affected the ANC considerably. First came the realisation that the uprising had happened without its intervention. Second, it had no resources on the ground to assist the young people who resisted with their lives. Third, it had to act quickly to gain mileage from this momentous event. And most important, it had to contend with a flood of young people who fled South Africa but who were determined to return to take up the fight, this time with guns in their hands. The simple truth was that the ANC was not prepared for the influx of young, energetic, committed school children who knew very little about the history and the policies of the ANC. They were housed in camps in Tanzania and Angola which were hardly adequate and offered little glamour or comfort. Boredom set in, followed by disillusionment. Soon there were accusations of drunkenness and sexual improprieties. These new recruits were only interested in military training and then returning to South Africa. But neither MK nor the political leadership was able to respond to these understandable ambitions. Instead, they imposed harsh discipline, which only served to increase frustration and lack of morale.

In 1979 the Report of the Politico-Military Strategy Commission (also known as the Green Book) was presented to the executive committee of the ANC. The commission was appointed after a visit by the ANC leadership to Vietnam in 1978, and started its work immediately, the executive having concluded that 'The Vietnam experience reveals certain shortcomings on our part and draws attention to areas of crucial importance which we have tended to neglect.'[12] The commission, which included Oliver Tambo, Thabo Mbeki, Joe Slovo, Moses Mabhida, Joe Gqabi and Joe Modise, held consultations with Reg September, Yusuf Dadoo, Chris Hani, Jack

Simons and Mac Maharaj of the SACP, as well as members of the ANC Women's Section and the ANC Youth and Student Section. The findings were far-reaching:

> It is necessary for our movement itself to entertain no ambiguities about the aims of the people's power and the role of the primary social forces, both inside and outside our movement, which will undertake these aims. … And we believe that there can be no true liberation without social emancipation. The Seizure of Power by the people must be understood not only by us but also by the masses as the beginning of the process in which the instruments of the State will be used to progressively destroy the heritage of all forms of national and social inequality.[13]

In terms of future strategy, the choice was between viewing the seizure of power as a general nation-wide insurrection which a period of armed struggle would have helped to stimulate, and the seizure of power 'through a protracted people's war in which partial and general uprisings will play a vital role'.[14] The second option gained maximum support. Spelling this out, the commission emphasised:

> … the strategic objective of our struggle is the Seizure of Power by the people as the first step in the struggle for the victory of our national democratic revolution. Seizure of Power by the people means and pre-supposes the all-round defeat of the fascist regime by the revolutionary forces of our country. It means the dismantling by the popular power of all the political, economic, cultural and other formations of racist rule and also necessitates the smashing of the state machinery of fas-cism and racism and the construction of a new one committed to the defence and advancement of the people's cause.[15]

Like Slovo's 'Strategy and Tactics' 10 years earlier, the commission fur-ther proposed that a major emphasis should be on political organisa-tion and mobilisation and that the armed struggle was secondary at this stage. However, it qualified this by stressing that MK should 'concentrate on armed propaganda actions, that is, armed action whose immediate purpose is to support and stimulate political activity and organisation rather than to hit at the enemy'.[16]

The recommendations were far-reaching but once again revealed the ambiguity within the leadership as to the role of the armed struggle. There was clearly a division between those who appreciated that the armed struggle on its own could not achieve victory and those who felt that a military solution should dominate strategy. The recommendations were also extremely important because of the calibre of the committee and the fact that the executive approved the commission's report in August 1979 in Dar es Salaam. As a consequence, the ANC's focus changed from a military struggle to a concentration on creating and building an underground movement. Nevertheless, armed attacks on key targets in South Africa took on a new significance. An example of this was the spectacular attack on three Sasol oil-from-coal plants in June 1980.

*　*　*

The mobilisation of above-ground and underground forces only really began in the 1980s under the banner of the United Democratic Front, which was formed in 1983 from over 500 student and youth organisations, trade unions, 'civics', women's organisations and church groups. As in the case of the Soweto uprising, the ANC in exile was not the prime mover, although a number of the UDF leaders owed their allegiance to the ANC. These included Oscar Mpetha, Archie Gumede and Albertina Sisulu. To avoid being banned by the state, the UDF leadership refrained from publicly declaring allegiance to the ANC. Similarly, the ANC in exile cautioned that furthering the aims of the ANC was a crime and therefore the UDF should avoid claiming any linkage with them. Although the UDF accepted the Freedom Charter as its guiding principle, the ANC in exile proposed that they should refrain from highlighting this, in order not to deter non-Charterists from supporting the UDF.

Despite the risks involved, key members of the UDF kept in touch with the movement in exile. What the ANC could not accomplish themselves had now come to pass and they gladly accepted this strengthening of their base inside South Africa.

CHAPTER TWO

A Government in Waiting: Exile in the 1980s

The situation has within it the potential for a relatively rapid emergence of conditions which make possible seizure of power. We cannot, however, be dogmatic about the exact moment and form of such a breakthrough ... it will depend not only upon what we do but also upon what the enemy does, not only on our strength but upon the enemy's weakness.

— SACP 7th CONGRESS, 1989

From survival mode in the 1960s, through the turbulent 1970s, the third decade in exile saw a more structured, more confident ANC in exile. The movement began to emerge as a 'government in waiting'. This is not to suggest that it was all plain sailing. The tensions and divisions remained. The South African security forces were better armed, better trained and ruthless, but within the ANC there was a greater cohesion and a greater confidence.

From very small beginnings, the exiled movement had grown into an organisation to be reckoned with; the international community was beginning to recognise the ANC as the legitimate liberation force in bringing about fundamental change in South Africa.

The United Nations had been supportive from very early on. Most of the support came from the General Assembly, which could only make recommendations, and they were very often vetoed by the Security Council, with the USA stigmatising the ANC as a terrorist organisation. So cooperation between the UN and the ANC was constantly a struggle. However, the UN very early on introduced an arms embargo and later supported boycotts and sanctions against South Africa, including a sports boycott and economic sanctions. It published support for the ANC

and recorded the incidence of racial segregation and attacks on democratic opposition within South Africa, as well as establishing a Trust Fund
and urging member countries to give (non-military) aid which enabled the
ANC to financially support its organisation outside the country. UN publications, videos and radio programmes gave greater credence to the claim
that the ANC was the legitimate 'government in waiting'.

On 21 August 1985 a Security Council statement read: 'the members of
the Council believe that a just and lasting solution in South Africa must be
based on the total eradication of the system of apartheid, and the establishment of a free, united and democratic society in South Africa'.[1]

However, it was not only the United Nations that supported the struggle
against apartheid. Through the influence of the SACP, a linkage had been
made very early on between the ANC and the Soviet Union. The Soviet
Union was the biggest financial supporter of the ANC for many years
until much later on, in the 1980s, Sweden became the largest contributor.[2]
But it was not only financial support that came from the Soviet bloc. They
offered military training in the Soviet Union and in East Germany and
a number of scholarships for young people who had fled South Africa.
These included university and college education in Moscow and in East
Germany as well as in the United Kingdom.

It was no life of luxury for the students, however. I recall visiting Moscow
in 1987 for discussions with political leaders and diplomats about the situation in South Africa. I received a request to meet with a group of young
black South African students. We met and I was dismayed at their criticism
of the standard of education they were receiving, the poor quality of food
and, above all, what they regarded as the racism of the Russian people. It
seemed that racism was not only prevalent in South Africa but was alive
and well everywhere.

Significant support came from the Anti-Apartheid Movement,
which operated worldwide, but was strongest in the UK and in Ireland.
Demonstrations, conferences and publications drew the attention of thousands of people to the fate of the black majority in South Africa. The ANC
had very close links with the Anti-Apartheid Movement and this gave further support to their claim to be the major liberation force in South Africa.

Financial support from a wide variety of sources enabled the ANC to build up its organisational structures, particularly in Lusaka:

> The exiled ANC in 20 years had vastly expanded in size and complexity. Its budget had grown from a few thousand dollars a year to three-quarters of a million dollars in 1972 and 56 million dollars in 1982. By the early 1980s it was a major source of support for over 9 000 members, operated diplomatic missions in 32 countries on five continents, had arranged scholarships for more than a thousand refugee students scattered around the world, and owned a fleet of more than 100 vehicles. It operated a farm in Zambia and a school, the Solomon Mahlangu Freedom College, at Mazimbu near Morogoro in Tanzania. It employed mechanics, teachers and doctors as well as highly-trained specialists in counter-intelligence, sabotage and other aspects of unconventional warfare.[3]

In April 1979, Solomon Mahlangu, the first MK cadre to be executed by the state, had said, 'My blood will nourish the tree which will bear the fruits of freedom. Tell my people that I love them and that they must continue the struggle.'[4] It seemed as if his prophetic words were beginning to come true.

* * *

Inside South Africa, concerted action by the United Democratic Front was laying the groundwork for additional pressure on the state, which was desperately seeking to strengthen its control with half-measures such as the tricameral parliament first mooted in 1982. Long before Tambo demanded that 'South African should be made ungovernable', that process had already started through the combined efforts of hundreds of organisations which united under the banner of the UDF. Although the exiled ANC could not claim to have initiated this development, they had been in touch with some of the UDF leadership from early on and indeed, belatedly claimed credit for the effective work accomplished.

Despite the weaknesses of the MK efforts, their propaganda value was priceless. Every time there was an act of sabotage, however small or large, it encouraged blacks to believe that their liberation was that bit closer. In addition to boosting the morale of blacks, the sabotage actions also unsettled the comfortable feelings of the white minority, who once thought that the security forces were unassailable. Ironically, the funerals of slain guerrillas were opportunities for large gatherings of people who glorified those who had given their lives for the struggle and encouraged further resistance. Media coverage of the trials of captured MK soldiers was further encouragement to supporters both within and outside South Africa.

There was another side to the growing success story. The leadership of the ANC in exile was extremely authoritarian and intolerant of dissent. The top leadership was tight-knit, middle-aged and older, and was in large measure unwilling to listen to the criticism and complaints which came from the rank and file of the movement. When dissatisfaction with conditions in the overcrowded camps spilled over into rebellion, they acted swiftly and ruthlessly in putting down the threatened uprising. Severe beatings, imprisonment and even executions followed without fair trial. Even as late as 1984, seven MK guerrillas were executed by firing squad. It is true that security agents had infiltrated the ANC in exile, and that this resulted in mistrust, suspicion and even paranoia, but the actions of MK commander Joe Modise and others cannot be condoned. Innocent people were punished because any dissent was seen to be the work of informers. It is an ugly side of the ANC in exile which spoilt and even betrayed the hard work, the sacrifices and bravery of many.

The ANC did establish a commission of inquiry to investigate the persistent and serious complaints and criticism from its members living in the camps in Angola – the Stuart Commission of March 1984. However, the commission's conclusions and recommendations were not nearly as strong and tough as they should have been. They included:

> The leadership have the benefits of good food, cigarettes, alcohol and use their influence to seduce women. The rank and file have poor food, are often short of cigarettes, and alcohol is strictly forbidden.
>
> Bureaucracy has reached alarming levels. It is impossible to be in touch with leadership and nepotism by the leadership has led to opportunism and corruption.

> Destructive punishment has become the order of the day. In fact, some of those punished have been maimed and scarred for life and there have even been deaths ...[5]

There were claims that the disturbances in the camps were the work of enemy agents, but the commission reported that it 'had no doubt that enemy agents and other elements did exploit genuine grievances and fanned the disturbances at a certain stage. We have not uncovered any evidence that enemy agents organised the disturbances from the beginning.

'The camps in Angola are riddled with those who are labelled as "suspects". Some have been in this category for as long as eight years. For those amongst them who are innocent, life must be real hell, and it is a sad commentary on the efficiency of the security department ... that this should be so.'[6] Coupled with months and years of waiting without any action or adequate preparation to return to South Africa as armed combatants, this state of affairs nearly resulted in revolution in the camps.

One of the commission's strongest statements reports that it 'found conditions in some camps shocking, to say the least. Extremely poor quality of food, no fresh meat, vegetables or fruits for months; hardly any recreation facilities, low-level of cultural activities, poor tents, uniforms, boots, sports shoes, if any, no medicaments, corruption and fear is omnipresent.'[7]

Regrettably, despite these shocking findings, the commission's recommendations did not match the gravity of the situation. Recommendations did include 'the holding of a national conference, general amnesty to be granted to all mutineers, Andrew Masondo [the ANC's national commissar, who was held responsible for the breakdown in discipline], to be "redeployed", the reform of the security department to be undertaken, conditions to be improved and the elite privileges abolished.'[8]

Looking back, it all sounds very familiar. Commissions are appointed, redeployment takes place (having been disgraced in Angola, Andrew Masondo was soon to be a general in the SANDF) and deep-seated grievances continue to fester. It is astonishing that the ANC got away with these relatively mild recommendations; in the long term this approach, which haunted the ANC then, still haunts it today.

The hard question which must be faced years after liberation is: is the culture of suspicion, mistrust and intolerance still rife within the ANC, and does this account for the ANC government's unhappiness with the Constitutional Court, its constant criticism of the media and its contempt for parliament?

In his important book, *External Mission: The ANC in Exile,* Stephen Ellis reveals another side to the myth of nobility in the struggle against the apartheid state. He not only relates the cruel punishments inflicted on guerrillas who lived for years in camps in Tanzania and in Angola, but also refers to the criminality amongst certain elements of the ANC in exile. This includes car smuggling, smuggling of Mandrax and an unholy alliance with gangsters and even rogue elements within South Africa's security forces. This raises the additional question: was the criminality and the culture of corruption which occurred in exile a foreshadow of the criminality and corruption exhibited by some contemporary ANC government officials at every level? This question will be addressed in Chapter Seven.

Ellis has done South Africa a signal service by referring in great detail to the cruelty meted out to those who fell foul of ANC authorities. In particular he points to the summary execution of those who were presumed to be informers. He comes out strongly as the prosecutor and does this very well. But he shows little awareness of the constraints under which the ANC existed in exile. The ANC was a stateless state; there were no courts, no judges, no defence lawyers. This is not to condone in any way the excesses of an authoritarian ANC which saw informers behind every bush.

A single example of the anger and bitterness felt by those whose loved ones were executed by the ANC is contained in the evidence of Joe Seremane, who told the TRC of his horror when he heard of the execution of his brother, Timothy Tebogo (aka Mahamba), in Quatro camp:

> I come here to express the feeling of betrayal by compatriots and comrades. I want someone to come and tell me what my young brother actually did that he deserved to be shot like an animal, being put down after being brutally disfigured so that his best friends could not recognise him … why do you think we ran and volunteered to risk our lives, calling on your own for your own return home for justice, supporting you in your call to be treated under the Geneva Convention and you couldn't treat

your own that way ... suddenly nobody has ever come across this young Seremane, suddenly no-one has ever known him, suddenly no-one has a record to show the kind of trial he had. Was he defended? Was he not defended? And where was the accountability that he couldn't account to his people and say he is dead ... I have been on the island, I have gone through hell, I have been tortured, nearly lost my life ... I have seen what it means to be tortured, but when I think of Chief Timothy and compare the way he died to my suffering, my suffering is nothing.[9]

This was only one example of the many witnesses who appeared before the Truth and Reconciliation Commission in relation to the death of loved ones while in exile.

It should be stated that in 1991 the ANC itself set up the Skweyiya Commission of Inquiry, which reported to the ANC president, to investigate allegations made by a group of 32 concerning poor conditions, maltreatment and the loss or destruction of property in the ANC detention camps. The Skweyiya Commission sat for several months and finally submitted its report, but it was an internal report and did not assign individual responsibility for abuses within the ANC, nor did it analyse the chains of command within the security department and MK, or between those bodies and the ANC leadership in order to establish political responsibility for what happened in the camps.

In 1993, as a result of dissatisfaction with the findings of the Skweyiya Commission, President Nelson Mandela appointed the independent Motsuenyane Commission of Inquiry, whose terms of reference were much broader than those of its predecessor. The commission held public hearings and heard evidence from 50 witnesses in Johannesburg. Its report found that there was a lack of accountability for excesses both at the Quatro camp and during the investigation of alleged enemy agents. It found further that the leadership did not deal adequately with the concerns and complaints of the so-called mutineers. The commission concluded that with the completion of its report, the ANC's task was only half done: 'Indeed, the victims of the abuses catalogued here have now been heard but in the view of the commission they have not yet received the full measure of justice due to them.'

Responding to the commission, the ANC national executive told the TRC that it 'deeply regrets the excesses' that took place. 'Further, we acknowledge that the real threat we faced and the difficult conditions under which we had to operate led to a drift in accountability and control away from established norms resulting in situations in which some individuals within the movement began to behave as a law unto themselves.'

But not all within the ANC were ready to apologise. General Masondo was asked for his view of the Motsuenyane Commission's recommendation that there be an apology made to the people who were wronged. He responded, 'People who it was found that they were enemy agents, we executed them. I wouldn't make an apology. We were at war. If it can be proved they were executed wrongly, I would be stupid not to say I apologise. But once people were threatening, the people who killed some of our comrades, I can't be apologetic that they were executed. Then I wouldn't be doing justice to those comrades who died.'

The TRC's finding was as follows: 'The relatively low number of violations and the limited extent to which they occurred demonstrated that torture was not a policy of the ANC. The commission nonetheless finds that the use of torture was unacceptable, whatever the circumstances. There are no extenuating circumstances for torture; there is no cause which is so just that torture can be justified in fighting for it.'

In August 2013, I listened to former judge Albie Sachs speaking at a workshop in Cape Town in August 2013. He has a marvellous ability to tell stories, but some of them are quite horrific. He referred to a meeting held with Oliver Tambo at Peace House in London in 1967 and related that Tambo had told him with deep sorrow and anguish, 'They [meaning the security forces] have made us into killers.' This is a very chilling statement, coming from the acting president of the ANC. In a further meeting with Tambo in 1987, Sachs said that Tambo acknowledged that torture had taken place, that he was deeply disturbed by it and wanted some kind of code of conduct to be recorded. Sachs was asked to draft such a code, which he did, and it would appear that as a direct result torture was stopped, executions no longer took place and discipline was carried out in terms of the Geneva Convention.

It is clear that there was a great deal of brutality within the ANC during the period of exile. It is also true that they conducted inquiries into these incidents of torture and brutality, and did not wait for the national Truth and Reconciliation Commission. It is also a fact that the then deputy president, Thabo Mbeki, together with several of his colleagues, apologised to the TRC as well as to the people of South Africa for the indiscipline, poor treatment and executions that had taken place, particularly during the 1960s and 1970s. Ellis never acknowledges the public apology offered by the ANC leadership. It is rare for a resistance movement anywhere to apologise for atrocities committed during a struggle for liberation.

* * *

In 1985, the ANC held a national conference in Kabwe, Zambia. A significant decision was taken by the conference to extend open membership to include the national executive. The new executive included five non-Africans, namely Joe Slovo, Aziz Pahad, James Stuart, Mac Maharaj and Reg September. At long last, the chief decision-making body included not only Africans but Indian, white and coloured members. Regrettably, little attention was paid to the complaints and grievances from ordinary members who still lived in overcrowded camps. Despite this, the mood of the conference was upbeat and much more militant. Despite the military superiority of the security forces, MK actions within South Africa grew exponentially. In 1985, there were 137 incidents of guerrilla action, up from 45 in 1984.

In demanding the intensification of the armed struggle, the distinction between 'soft' and 'hard' targets seemed to be abandoned. Tambo expressed regret at the killing of civilians through guerrilla actions, but pointed out that black civilians were being killed daily by the security forces. In later years, the Truth and Reconciliation Commission acknowledged the grave concern of the ANC's national executive and Tambo in particular. Nevertheless, the commission stated, 'It is equally clear that action was rarely taken against operatives or units who were responsible for these breaches of humanitarian law.'[10]

While optimism was running high, it is improbable that any of those attending the Kabwe Conference believed that in five years' time the ANC leadership would be at the negotiating table with hated apartheid leaders. 'Seizure of power' was still the watchword, but now more than ever it would come about by not only military action but also political organisation, with primacy given to politics rather than military strategy. At Kabwe, no consideration was given to negotiating with the enemy.

However, in the latter half of 1985, there was a discernible shift towards the possibility of a negotiated settlement. This is true not only of the ANC in exile, but also amongst their supporters in South Africa. The idea had even begun to surface in the minds of the apartheid government, and would soon lead to the beginnings of discussions between Nelson Mandela and the minister of justice, Kobie Coetsee. But this was a slow process and neither side really wanted a negotiated settlement; each wanted absolute victory. A genuine commitment to negotiation would only occur when both sides recognised that the conflict itself had reached stalemate proportions. The ANC did not have the military strength to overthrow a sophisticated army; neither did the apartheid government have the power to halt the ever-increasing opposition from outside and inside South Africa, despite the increased powers given to the security forces under the State of Emergency imposed by PW Botha in July 1985. The government was beginning to buckle under the pressure from the international community. Sanctions had bitten deeply, but with the Chase Manhattan Bank's refusal to roll over South Africa's loans, and the change in relationship between the United States and the ANC, the writing was on the wall.

Two further significant events influenced the government's thinking. In November 1985, the Congress of South African Trade Unions (Cosatu) was established, bringing together more than 700 000 workers under a single organising umbrella. This raised the stakes considerably and increased the intensity of protest. The second event occurred in August 1987 when the National Union of Mineworkers (NUM) went to war with the all-powerful Chamber of Mines. There was a nation-wide strike by 250 000 black miners, which lasted for three weeks. NUM was forced to call off the strike but the miners were reinstated and major concessions were made by the mining houses. The unions and the UDF joined forces in many of the protests throughout the country, and the confidence which was once a hallmark of the South African government began to falter.

* * *

In January 1985 PW Botha offered Mandela release on condition he renounced the armed struggle. The prospect of discussions between Mandela and the government resulted in a great deal of anxiety within the ANC in exile. There was very little communication and they began to wonder whether Mandela was selling out in making far-reaching decisions on his own. This was never the case, but the suspicions remained for a long time and Mandela had to do everything in his power to ensure that the movement both inside and outside the country recognised his total allegiance to the ANC and understood that he would never strike a deal without the consent of the movement.

Most of these suspicions were put to rest by a speech by Zindzi Mandela at Jabulani Amphitheatre in Soweto on 10 February 1985 – significantly, at a UDF rally to celebrate the award of the Nobel Peace Prize to Archbishop Desmond Tutu. This is in part his reply to PW Botha's offer, which his daughter read out to a large gathering: 'Throughout our struggle there have been puppets who have claimed to speak for you. They have made this claim both here and abroad. They are of no consequence. My father and his colleagues will not be like them. My father says, "I am a member of the African National Congress. I have always been a member of the African National Congress and I will remain a member of the African National Congress until the day I die."'

Mandela's reply also refers to the many instances when he and his party had asked successive National Party leaders for 'a round table conference to find a solution to the problems of our country, but they were all ignored'. He then asks Botha to show that he is different from his predecessors. 'Let him renounce violence. Let him say he will dismantle apartheid … Only free men can negotiate. Prisoners cannot enter into contracts.'

Zindzi concluded her speech by stating, 'My father says "I cannot and will not give any undertaking at a time when I and you, the people, are not free. Your freedom and mine cannot be separated. I will return."'

*　　*　　*

1985 also saw the beginning of the visits by mainly white South African individuals and institutions to the ANC in Lusaka for discussions and debate.
The first delegation of business leaders and newspaper editors was headed
by Gavin Relly of the powerful Anglo American Corporation. This took
place on 13 September 1985. The business community tried to persuade
the ANC to accept the idea of a national convention movement, which
was first formulated by the Progressive Federal Party. Although the ANC
didn't accept this overture, the discussions were cordial.

In mid-October of the same year, a delegation from the Progressive
Federal Party, comprising Van Zyl Slabbert, Colin Eglin, Peter Gastrow
and myself, visited Lusaka. We spent several days in discussion with key
ANC leaders, in particular with Thabo Mbeki. We discussed the possibility of a negotiated settlement and we asked questions about the economic
and social policies of the ANC. Again, while the discussions were warm
and friendly, there was no real acceptance of the need to end the armed
struggle and to meet at the negotiating table with the South African government. I recall Mac Maharaj questioning me closely about where I was
born, about my parents, about my life and what I had done. When I had
told him my story, he said with a very broad grin, 'Ah, I see you are a true
liberal idealist.' My reply was, yes I was an idealist and I hoped that he too
had ideals and that together, inside and outside South Africa, we could
make these ideals come true.

Our relationship with Thabo Mbeki was particularly warm and we
followed up later by arranging the widely publicised visit to Dakar in
Senegal. This was in 1987, after Van Zyl Slabbert and I had resigned from
parliament and started a new organisation, the Institute for a Democratic
Alternative for South Africa (Idasa). There are those who suggest that the
ANC persuaded Van Zyl to leave parliament. They certainly put pressure
on him, but long before our visit to Lusaka, he and I had discussed the possibility of leaving parliament. It was clear that Thabo Mbeki in particular

34

was keen that Slabbert and others should leave parliament as a protest against an all-white institution that refused to come to terms with the majority of people in South Africa.

There is a very interesting letter written by Mbeki to Slabbert, which has never been published. My recollection is that Slabbert only received that letter on the very day he announced his resignation during the No Confidence debate (he had informed Mbeki in advance of his intention). The letter (*see pages 36–37*) makes interesting reading.[11]

Slabbert was pleased that the ANC and Mbeki in particular were concerned with white opposition to apartheid and did not dismiss his leaving parliament as a non-event. But he was quick to make it very clear that his decision to resign was not the result of pressure from the ANC but was made independently. Both Slabbert and I were uncomfortable with being members of parliament long before we met with Mbeki, and especially after the tricameral parliament was established.

The Dakar visit was much more public than many other initiatives that were undertaken by various individuals and groups. A year or two later, there were serious discussions between the NIS (National Intelligence Service), led by Professor Willie Esterhuyse of Stellenbosch University, and Thabo Mbeki and others. These discussions took place at Mells Park in the United Kingdom (there were persistent rumours that Esterhuyse was linked with the NIS before they approached him to lead the delegation to meet with the ANC). This was followed by direct discussions between the NIS and the ANC in Switzerland. The visits to Lusaka started as a trickle but became almost a flood. According to Professor Emeritus Michael Savage, there were at least 137 visits to the ANC between 1983 and 1990. According to Savage, one of the first was the late Archbishop Denis Hurley, who met with Oliver Tambo for three hours in the Paddington Hotel in London.

The pressure to negotiate was now on the ANC. After nearly 30 years in exile, it was clear that the way was opening for the first attempts at a settlement.

* * *

Our Thinking

The decision you have **taken** has the pontential to make a very important impact towards the kind of society which we all seek. We think it is therefore very important that your announcement should measure up to the importance of the occasion.

It is necessary that you emerge as the man of vision whom it is said is lacking in white politics. To emerge as such a man it is vital that you make a clean break both with the institution where you will be speaking and the system of which it is part.

It is necessary to state and proceed from the position that the system cannot be reformed. Therefore you should avoid giving any impression that if certain elements were to be removed then the system would be more or less acceptable.

Concerning the methods of change, it would be important to raise the issue of the right and duty to rebel against tyranoy. You personally would of course express that rebellion using peaceful means. It is also crucial that the distinction be made between the violence of the tyrant and the response of the tyranised. It is equally necessary to affirm that the time is past when the definition and pace of change can be made exclusively by those who enjoy tyranical power. It also needs to be said that negotiations are necessitated exactly by the fact that people have defferent views. To insist that some should ammend their views before negotiations can take place is to ask not for negotiations but for surrender.

As to your future conduct it would be important to say that you can only sit as a representative in a democratic institution. For present purposes, you could stand again on a democratic platform and, when elected, not take your seat.

It would be good if you could speak also as an Afrikaner and project your position, correctly as one that seeks the security of the Afrikaner people. You should contest P.W. B's claim in this regard and advance a vision of an afrikaner who will be African and therefore happy to live as an equal and at peace with other Africans regardless of race and colour.

../2

36

- 2 -

The end result has to be that you emerge as a leader of all the people of
our country. For that to happen you have to be seen to be advancing the
cause of genuine democracy and justice for all. We are confident that
you will live up to the tasks which history has imposed on us all.

Regards

Jan. 1986

Reproduced with kind permission from former President Thabo Mbeki.

With the proliferation of talks, and talks about talks, between Mandela and government while he was still in prison, the highly publicised Dakar talks, talks in England between leading ANC officials and the Esterhuyse delegation, Tambo decided that he had to take the initiative. In 1989 he had discussions with delegations from the Mass Democratic Movement (which had formed after the banning of the UDF, and included Cosatu) on the drafting of a document which would clearly set out the demands of the ANC if negotiations were to take place. The pace of talks began to increase and meetings were held with the OAU, with the ANC insisting that this document should have the backing of both the OAU and the international community. The OAU agreed and gave the ANC two weeks to prepare such a document.

Tambo, together with several colleagues, spent days flying around the world seeking support for the draft of the document. On 21 August 1989, a special OAU sub-committee met with the ANC in Harare and they accepted what became known as the Harare Declaration. It is worth quoting from the Statement of Principles and the Climate for Negotiations.[12]

The Principles include the following:

> [The OAU] are at one with [the majority of the people of South Africa] that the outcome of such a process should be a new constitutional order based on the following principles, amongst others:

> - South Africa should become a united, democratic and non-racial state.
> - All its people shall enjoy common and equal citizenship and nationality, regardless of race, colour, sex or creed.
> - All its people should have the right to participate in the government and administration of the country on the basis of universal suffrage, exercised through one person, one vote, under a common voters' roll.
> - All shall have the right to form and join any political party of their choice provided that it is not in furtherance of racism.
> - All shall enjoy universally recognised human rights, freedoms and civil liberties, protected under an entrenched bill of rights.
> - South Africa shall have a new legal system which shall guarantee equality of all before the law.

- South Africa shall have an independent and non-racial judiciary.
- There shall be created an economic order which shall promote and advance the wellbeing of all South Africans.

Under the heading of 'Climate for Negotiations' were the following demands:

- Release all political prisoners and detainees unconditionally and refrain from imposing any restrictions on them.
- Lift all bans and restrictions on all proscribed and restricted organisations and people.
- Remove all troops from the townships.
- End the state of emergency and repeal all legislation, such as, and including, the Internal Security Act, designed to circumscribe political activity.
- Cease all political trials and political executions.

It is interesting that the Harare Declaration included a demand for 'the formation of an interim government to supervise the process of the drawing up and adoption of a new constitution; govern and administer the country, as well as effect the transition to a democratic order, including the holding of elections'.

The Declaration also states that 'after the adoption of the new constitution, all armed hostilities will be deemed to have been formally terminated and for its part, the international community would lift the sanctions that have been imposed against apartheid South Africa'.

* * *

Despite the growing confidence within the exiled movement that negotiations were a distinct possibility, there was also considerable doubt and suspicion in case they let their guard down and were betrayed by President de Klerk and his government. After decades of distrust, there were many in the ANC who felt they were walking into a trap. Thus they took out a couple of insurance policies. First, the armed struggle would continue. This, they believed, would keep the pressure on the government. It would also maintain the high morale amongst black South Africans. Second, they were determined to strengthen their underground presence in South Africa. This would draw them into closer cooperation with the UDF and other formations in preparation for their return, if negotiations became a reality. It would also be a growing force in case the negotiations went very badly wrong.

This latter move, the strengthening of the underground movement, brought about Operation Vula, which was first discussed as early as 1986. Central to this idea of creating a firm base inside the country were Jacob Zuma, Chris Hani, Joe Slovo and Mac Maharaj. Tambo was part of the deliberations from the beginning. However, Mac Maharaj was chiefly responsible for the success of the infiltration. With great bravery and daring, bearing in mind his previous incarceration in prison and horrific torture, he planned the operation and he returned secretly to South Africa on 31 July 1988. The preparations and the re-entry read like a James Bond thriller: wigs, make-up, special clothing, codes, forged ID documents, secret assignations, training in Moscow and Cuba, and a highly sophisticated system of communication. So clever were the communications that Maharaj and his team brought Mandela and Tambo into direct contact even while Mandela was in prison.

But the security police finally caught up with Maharaj and he was arrested on 25 July 1990. The announcement of his arrest and the disclosure of secret documents and arms caches, which seemed to point towards a communist plot to sabotage the negotiations, caused a huge outcry. The media had a field day. Accusations and counter-accusations flew in every direction. White South Africans believed that this was a communist plot from the very beginning and were distrustful of the negotiations.

Mac Maharaj and his key operatives (including Pravin Gordhan, the current minister of finance!) were charged with terrorism in terms of section 54 of the Internal Security Act. The trial dragged on for months – and then, out of the blue, the prosecution announced that President de Klerk had granted immunity to all eight.

Both parties were to face many serious challenges during the next four years of on-off negotiations. At last, an Interim Constitution was agreed upon and – after a referendum – a date set for South Africa's first-ever democratic election, on 27 April 1994. The ANC won with a large majority and Mandela the prisoner became Mandela the president.

* * *

In the first two chapters, I have raised several disturbing questions about the ANC in exile. We need to look more closely at the possible links between these questions and the ANC in government today.

- Does the oft-quoted goal of seizure of power still exist in the minds of the leadership of the ANC and the SACP? Is the eventual aim a one-party state?
- Does the culture of suspicion, mistrust and extreme intolerance that existed within the ANC ranks in exile account for the ANC government's disenchantment with the Constitutional Court, its constant criticism of the media and its contempt for parliament? Did the 30 years in exile create the climate that still exists today?
- Was the criminality and the culture of corruption which occurred in exile a foreshadow of the criminality and corruption exhibited by many contemporary ANC government officials today at every level?

There are additional questions. Bureaucracy seems to have been the hallmark of leadership during the period of exile. This made it difficult for ordinary members to break through into any meaningful communication with a tight-knit group at the top. Is this still a characteristic of the ANC today? The high life of the leadership in contrast to the rank and file was bitterly criticised in exile, and this distinction is true today. Further, there is the evidence that there was maladministration, wrong choices, deployment of people to tasks for which they had little training or qualifications. This seems to be the pattern today – and the question is, yet again, is this a continuation of how the ANC operated in exile?

A further issue which seemed to be at the heart of many of the mistakes made in exile was political incoherence. There were clearly strong divisions between those who believed that the way to overthrow apartheid and bring about an ANC government was insurrection and the armed struggle, and those who believed that the armed struggle in itself was not sufficient and a far greater emphasis ought to be on political organisation, not merely in exile but in South Africa itself. There seemed to be a wide divergence of opinion in the ANC as to its political plan, both then and for the future. Can it be that the divisions so evident in exile are still rife today?

A final question would have to deal with the influence of the South African Communist Party. Clearly the party was very influential in the decision to shift from passive resistance to the armed struggle. Furthermore, the SACP was far better organised in the early years of exile than the ANC, and was instrumental in linking the ANC with the Soviet Union and East Germany. It is well known that many of the ANC leaders, perhaps all of them, were at one time or another also members of the South African Communist Party. The accusation of 'Stalinist' is still frequently applied to key figures, and can be seen in intolerance of opposition, an inclination to suppress dissident views, and concentration of power in one person. How strong is the party's influence today?

This, coupled with the influence of Cosatu in the tripartite alliance, must also be interrogated. It is difficult to gauge just how strong the influence of these two partners is, because their meetings are never held in public and there are no formal announcements of decisions taken, but it is easy to read between the lines that there are some real divisions and in the end, one has to wonder who is calling the shots, who is running South Africa. Is it the ANC, the South African Communist Party, Cosatu, or a combination of all three?

To demonstrate whether or not these far-reaching issues and features were still pertinent after the ANC was elected as government will require in the first instance a consideration of the government's view of the separation of powers, and the party's attitude towards parliament as the legislature, which the following chapters will address.

CHAPTER THREE

Parliament: Legislator or Lame Duck?

The national assembly is elected to represent the people and to ensure government by the people under the Constitution. It does this by choosing the president, by providing a national forum for public consideration of issues, by passing legislation and by scrutinising and overseeing executive action.
— CONSTITUTION OF THE REPUBLIC OF SOUTH AFRICA, CHAPTER 4

I served as the member of parliament for Pinelands for 12 years, from 1974 to 1986, when I decided to leave parliament in a somewhat abrupt way. My resignation was preceded by a growing sense of futility at the overwhelming majority enjoyed and exploited by the National Party. As an opposition, we won the debates but this counted for nothing when the voting took place. However, the main reason for walking out of parliament was the amendment to the Constitution and the introduction of the tricameral parliament, which had two major flaws. There was a built-in white majority, which meant that the coloured and Indian chambers could never outvote whites on any key or critical issue. But much more importantly, the party that I represented, the Progressive Federal Party, argued against the exclusion of black South Africans. We warned that this would only exacerbate a situation that had already provoked major conflict within the country and that blacks would become even angrier and more robust in their opposition to apartheid policies.

The National Party campaign for the tricameral parliament had been built around the catch phrase that it would be a 'step in the right direction'. Relieved and confused, white voters bought the argument and gave President PW Botha a two-thirds majority. The National Party was understandably cock-a-hoop. We, on the other hand, were deeply depressed. We knew beyond a shadow of a doubt that the exclusion of blacks would only pour fuel on an already smouldering and resentful mood.

Ironically, a direct consequence of this new Constitution, which excluded blacks, was the birth of the United Democratic Front, which harnessed civil society to such an extent that the pressure on the government increased a hundred-fold. A united, active civil society was far more effective in forcing the National Party to the negotiation table than the opposition in parliament.

From my point of view, the overwhelming support for the government from the electorate called for some radical action by the Progressive Federal Party. I discussed this with Harry Pitman at our annual party congress. He supported the idea of our taking a much bolder stand. Tragically, he collapsed and died from a heart attack during the congress. When I discussed with Van Zyl Slabbert the idea that we should resign our seats and fight the by-elections on the absolute necessity to include blacks in a parliamentary system, he urged caution. He said that he had discussed this idea with Helen Suzman, but she felt that we should at least give the new system a chance before rejecting it outright. She was strongly of the view that parliament still had an important role to play and that the PFP's presence there was essential.[1] Suffice to say, Slabbert walked out of parliament at the end of the no-confidence debate in February 1986 and I followed a week later.

During the writing of this book, in 2012, I planned to interview a number of parliamentarians and political party leaders and I wanted permission to enter parliament on a regular basis. I wrote to the secretary of parliament requesting authorisation to attend both the national assembly and committee meetings on a regular basis rather than asking for a pass each time I wanted to enter the building. To my surprise, I received a letter from him informing me that as an ex-member of parliament, I could visit any time I wished to. He asked only that I make application so that I could be given a photo ID enabling me to visit without any further permission. I also talked with an old friend, Wilmot James, my successor at Idasa when I left that organisation in 1994, who is chairman of the Democratic Alliance. He gave me some good advice, because I knew almost nothing of the layout of the new building, while his secretary furnished me with the phone numbers and email addresses of most of the parliamentarians.

I made my way to the parliamentary building for the first time since I had walked out in 1986. I saw an entirely different scene. I sat in the gallery and looked down, deeply impressed and moved by a vision of multiculturalism and diversity. It was clear from the gallery that the ANC dominated, but the whole scene seemed to be more relaxed (in fact, so relaxed that several members were fast asleep). Instead of the dark suits that we wore, many of the men were without jackets and few were wearing ties. It looked a more modern and obviously much more representative parliament than I had known. The building itself is much larger, to accommodate many more members of parliament representing the entire country. It is a very modern, well-structured and suitable venue for a modern, striving new democracy.

I also took the opportunity to attend some of the committee meetings. These were very different from the ones which I had experienced. In the old white parliament, we did most of our work in the plenary sessions. There were special committees appointed from time to time to consider each bill, but not on a regular basis. I was impressed by the attention to detail by the representative structure of each committee that I visited, and in many instances the tone of the debate was very high. However, it was clear to me that each party had two or three members who were up to date and knew the subject, while the rest seemed to be uninterested passengers. Nevertheless, the committee system at its best is a great improvement on what I experienced in my time in parliament. The potential is there for rigorous debate and the meetings are open to the public and hence to the media.

In my regular visits to parliament, I constantly asked myself the question: what is the constitutional responsibility of parliament in terms of the separation of powers into executive, legislature (that is, parliament) and judiciary? I am therefore going to deal first with what the Constitution demands of parliament before looking in Chapter Four at the role which parliamentarians had defined for themselves.

* * *

The Constitution is unambiguous: parliament is subservient to the Constitution and therefore the first loyalty of members of that body is to the Constitution, not to themselves or their party. In Chapter 4, under the heading, 'National Legislative Authority' (4), the Constitution states, 'When exercising its legislative authority, parliament is bound only by the Constitution, and must act in accordance with, and within the limits of, the Constitution.' And paragraph 48 of Chapter 4 states, 'Before members of the national assembly begin to perform their functions in the assembly, they must swear or affirm faithfulness to the Republic and obedience to the Constitution, in accordance with Schedule 2.'

Despite the strong and clear injunctions contained in the Constitution, the ANC at the very outset made it clear that the first allegiance of their members of parliament is to the party rather than to the Constitution or to parliament. This despite the fact that all members take an oath of obedience to the Constitution. The 1994 code of conduct for ANC MPs declares, 'All elected members shall be under the constitutional authority of the highest decision-making bodies of the ANC, and decisions and policies of the highest ANC organs shall take precedence over all other structures, including ANC structures in parliament and government.' It also forbids MPs from 'the attempt to make use of the parliamentary structures to undermine organisational decisions and policies'.[2] Any ANC member of parliament who disregards this could face a disciplinary hearing, could be removed from parliament, even in the middle of their elected term, could be redeployed, or could face censure by not being placed on the party list in a forthcoming election. This means that ANC members of parliament are loath to contradict the party leadership, even when their conscience and the oath they took suggests that they should vote differently from what is being proposed by the ANC caucus in parliament.

Gareth van Onselen's definition of cadre deployment gives some useful background here:

> The appointment by government, at the behest of the governing party,
> of a party-political loyalist to an institution or body, independent or
> otherwise, as a means of circumventing public reporting lines and
> bringing that institution under the control of the party, as opposed to

the state. Cadre deployment, a longstanding idea with a very particular ideological history, involves the creation of a parallel power structure to the constitution, so that party members answer first to the party, second to the public. In turn, that the party might advance its interests ahead of those of the public.[3]

To ensure that ANC policies are strictly adhered to, the party has set up structures that determine which policies are going to be presented in parliament, and how their elected parliamentarians should vote. This is done firstly through the national executive, which is chaired by the president of the ANC – and in this instance we have President Jacob Zuma, who is president of the country as well as of the party. In this he follows Thabo Mbeki, who insisted on very strong centralised organisation to ensure that the ruling party carried out its policies. There is also the National Working Committee (NWC) of the ANC, which considers day-to-day policy. Remarkably, the NWC, which doesn't even meet in Cape Town, sets the agenda for parliament and conveys this to the party's chief whip. The ANC parliamentary caucus meets once a week to discuss the proposals put forward by the NWC, and while there is a measure of debate and opportunity for questions to be put, it is very rare that the caucus will differ from these recommendations.

It is clear that the real decisions are made firstly in the NWC, then in its parliamentary caucus and then in the ANC committee study groups. This means that even though the parliamentary committee meetings are open to the public, most of the legislation and decision-making has been finalised by the party, which has an overwhelming majority both in parliament and in every committee. The NWC, to ensure that its instructions are carried out, appoints the chairs of all the parliamentary committees as well as the deputy speaker and the speaker. Control is thus the name of the game and very much in the hands of the ANC. Parliament is subservient to the wishes and control of Luthuli House and the question can rightly be posed: is it in effect a lame duck or a rubber stamp?

In an interview I had with Lindiwe Mazibuko, the Democratic Alliance parliamentary leader (September 2012), she agreed that in many senses parliament has become a lame duck. She believes it was under the presidency of Thabo Mbeki that power became centralised in the ANC and that parliament became subservient to the party executive and leadership. She stressed that the ANC majority prevails in every area of parliament so, despite the best efforts of the Democratic Alliance and other opposition parties, it is almost impossible to bring about substantial change.

On 27 May 2012, in an article in the *Sunday Times*, Ms Mazibuko acknowledged that: 'Parliament, its committees and individual members, for example, have the authority to summon ministers to account for the effective implementation of their policies.' But she goes on to say, 'Yet we rarely exercise this power. On the occasions that we do, ministers often dodge committee meetings like errant schoolchildren, choosing to delegate their responsibilities to directors-general … political accountability is therefore short-circuited, and committees cannot reprimand directors-general for policy failures because they have no mandate to do so.'

In an interview I had with ANC veteran Benjamin Turok in September 2012, he conceded that loyalty and commitment to the party supersede personal commitment and merit. He complained about the mediocrity of ANC MPs, which in his view stems largely from the belief amongst ANC members that parliament is not important and that they would be better off in a state department or in business rather than sitting in the national assembly. He admitted that very few MPs participate in the key debates in parliament and that the ANC in parliament is strongly controlled by the chief whip. He also conceded that at times in parliament, he is tugged in two directions: when he stands up to deliver a speech, he has to bear in mind both his loyalty to the party and also his commitment to the principles of democracy.

This is a startling statement from a long-time member of the ANC and the SACP, and indicates the power that the party has over parliament and its members. Turok, however, did stress the importance of the Ethics Committee, of which he is chair. The censuring of the former minister of communications, Dina Pule, in August 2013 justified to an extent his confidence in this committee. While some would see her temporary expulsion from parliament, the loss of one month's salary and having to make a formal apology in parliament as a slap on the wrist, it is nevertheless one of the strongest actions ever taken by the Ethics Committee against any member. The powers of the Ethics Committee need to be increased so that it can effectively censure and suspend members who are in conflict with the rules of parliament and those who lie to parliament.

Attendance by ANC members in parliament is deplorable. Time and time again, even the chief whip of the ANC has complained strongly, in public, that MPs are not in attendance as often as they ought to be. It is well known that Winnie Madikizela-Mandela is rarely seen in the parliamentary precincts, even though she has been an MP for many years. The Constitution is quite clear about what should happen to members who are absent from parliament. It states that 'A person loses membership of the national assembly if that person ... is absent from the Assembly without permission in circumstances for which the rules and orders of the Assembly prescribe loss of membership.' If the speaker, the chief whip and the ANC were serious, a large number of ANC MPs would lose their membership of the national assembly. The poor attendance is a reflection of how ANC members view the role and status of parliament. For them it is obviously not significant; there are other spheres of policy making and possibly of promotion, and even involvement in business dealings, which are more important than parliament.

An interview with Donwald Pressly, the *Cape Times* parliamentary correspondent, in June 2013, revealed a more pragmatic approach as to whether or not one could describe parliament as a lame duck. He felt strongly that the majoritarian system, which gave almost unlimited powers to the ANC majority, was the cause of the problem. The ruling party should make it easier for opposition parties to be more directly involved in procedural matters, in particular in the introduction of legislation. He felt that parliament as it exists today is not able to respond to the demands laid down by the Constitution. However, as a journalist, preoccupied with the freedom of the press, he was pleased that the rules of *Hansard* allowed speeches delivered both in plenary and in committee stage to be reported by the media.

* * *

The Constitution is equally clear about the election and role of the president as the executive authority of the Republic. In Chapter 5 of the Constitution, the responsibilities of the president are outlined:

> Section 85 (1) and (2): The executive authority of the Republic is vested in the president. The president exercises the executive authority together with other members of the cabinet by (a) implementing national legislation except where the Constitution or an act of parliament provides otherwise; (b) developing and implementing a national policy; (c) coordinating the functions of state departments and administrations; (d) preparing and initiating legislation; and (e) performing any other executive function provided for in the Constitution or in national legislation.

Thus, in terms of the Constitution, the president has awesome powers and responsibilities. But the Constitution goes on to set out the procedures for the removal of a president. In section 89 (1) and (2), the procedure is clearly set out:

> The national assembly, by a resolution adopted with the supporting vote of at least two thirds of its members, may remove the president from office only on the grounds of (a) a serious violation of the Constitution or the law, (b) serious misconduct; or (c) inability to perform the functions of the office.

The Constitution also states that, 'Anyone that has been removed from the office of president in terms of sub-sections 1(a) or (b) above, may not receive any benefits of that office, and may not serve in any public office.'

It is clear from the above that the decision by the national executive of the ANC to demand that President Thabo Mbeki resign the presidency was unconstitutional. The president is elected – and removed – by parliament, not by a political party. However, Mbeki was left with almost no choice. If he had decided to ignore or refuse the demand, there would have been a debate in parliament and a very uncomfortable and unpleasant constitutional crisis. In actual fact, it would have been better for him to have refused to resign so that this matter could have been debated in parliament in terms of the procedures set out above. But there were other forces at play, which placed overwhelming pressure on Mbeki to put the party above all else. It is doubtful whether the ANC could have secured a two-thirds majority if it went to a vote. Even if it had been successful, Mbeki could have appealed to the Constitutional Court, which would have ruled his sacking by the NEC as unconstitutional.

There are two possible reasons why President Mbeki decided to accept the harsh, ruthless decision of his own national executive. First, he is a child of the ANC. His father, the well-known Govan Mbeki, would have influenced him enormously. He went into exile aged 22 and served the ANC in many capacities and in leading positions for many years before he returned to South Africa in 1990. It would have been very difficult for him to oppose the party that he had served for so long. The pressure must have been horrendous. His decision may well be the best example of how the ANC puts party above parliament and indeed above the state.

The second possible reason is a more cynical one. If he had refused to go along with the demand of the NEC, in terms of the Constitution he would not receive any benefits of the office of the president and would not be able to serve in any public office. This may also have influenced his decision. Whatever, the reason – and perhaps there are others as well – there is no doubt that the sacking of Thabo Mbeki as president is a classic example of power politics and of the party being treated as superior to all other agencies or organisations. This is a further example of the ANC's contempt for the Constitution and for parliament.

It is clear from the Constitution that successive presidents, together with their cabinets, can accept praise for positive developments that have taken place while they have been in office. It is also clear that on the same basis, they must accept the responsibility for the lack of development in almost every area. Section 92 states that the deputy president and ministers 'are responsible for the powers and functions of the executive assigned to them by the president'. This means that they cannot simply point to the president and blame him for not carrying out the responsibilities imposed on him in terms of the Constitution.

The Constitution continues, 'Members of the cabinet are accountable collectively and individually to parliament for the exercise of their powers and the performance of their functions ... members of the cabinet must act in accordance with the Constitution and provide parliament with full and regular reports concerning matters under their control.'

Comments made almost daily by the members of opposition parties and in media reports indicate strongly that ministers and deputy ministers hold parliament in contempt. Time and time again, it is reported that they do not respond to requests from various committees for them to report on their responsibilities. Time and time again they send directors-general in their place. The collective responsibility of the president, the deputy president and cabinet ministers is clear, but unfortunately they do not individually or collectively seem to care what the opposition and many members of civil society have to say about their conduct or misconduct. They are a law unto themselves and this makes parliament a much poorer and more ineffective place. Needless to say, it would be difficult if not impossible for the opposition to make a case against the cabinet at the Constitutional Court for their ineptitude, inefficiency and contempt for parliamentary procedures.

A further example of the lack of respect by the cabinet for parliament is its attitude to questions. Questions are a vital part of parliamentary procedure and afford members of parliament and parties the opportunity to ask concrete and searching questions of the president and cabinet members. However, it is clear that in many instances a very long period elapses from the time the question is posed to its answer being tabled. In some instances, questions simply go unanswered. This is a slap in the face of democracy and makes it extraordinarily difficult for members of the opposition to hold the executive to account. There are almost no questions posed by ANC members, who are either uninterested or are nervous and even fearful of putting questions to the president, the deputy president or cabinet ministers.

* * *

There are many examples of the failure of parliament to oversee the executive. The most glaring is the manner in which parliament dismally failed in its attempt to hold responsible those implicated in the notorious so-called arms deal.

Under the leadership of Joe Modise, who was appointed minister of defence in 1994, Armscor proposed a deal to purchase a huge quantity of highly sophisticated and very costly weapons, including warships, fighter jets and submarines. The deal was sealed in 1999, a mere five years after the ANC became the government.

The spending of such vast sums of money that could otherwise have been spent on providing services to the poor was strongly criticised by the media, by civil society, by the Democratic Alliance and other opposition parties and even, initially, by some in the ANC. As early as 1994, when Armscor mooted the purchase of corvettes to the value of nearly R5 billion, Joe Slovo, then minister of housing, stated in parliament, 'An amount of R4.6 billion would allow us to provide housing subsidies to at least one and a half million people.' He was joined by Max Sisulu (who later became speaker of parliament) when he declared during the same parliamentary debate, 'There is certainly no external threat to our security. There is, however, an internal threat to our security and that comes from unemployment, poverty and deprivation. That is the enemy that we face, an enemy from within.' Despite this early criticism, parliament acceded to the Armscor proposal.

The question is, why did parliament fail so dismally to block this far-reaching decision, and why did it fail to provide oversight to the executive, which it is called to do by the Constitution? The story is well told by Andrew Feinstein in *After the Party* and by Paul Holden and Hennie van Vuuren in *The Devil in the Detail*. For our purposes, it is necessary only to highlight the process and underline the failure of parliament to fulfil its obligation to uphold the Constitution in terms of giving oversight to the executive, in other words, a strong, clear example of parliament being in danger of looking like a lame duck rather than the legislature at work.

In short (thanks to Paul Holden's *The Arms Deal in Your Pocket*), it all started when the Auditor-General requested permission to audit the arms deal, which was already subject to media speculation about corruption. Shortly thereafter Patricia de Lille, then a PAC MP, came into possession of a briefing document on the arms deal signed by 'concerned ANC MPs'.

After some difficulties raised by Thabo Mbeki, the audit went ahead and was submitted to parliament in August 2000. The report then came to the attention of Scopa, the Standing Committee on Public Accounts, the most powerful committee in parliament, chaired by Gavin Woods of the Inkatha Freedom Party, and including Andrew Feinstein, an ANC MP. Scopa's report, submitted in October 2000, called for a comprehensive investigation, to be headed up by Scopa but to include the Auditor-General, the Office for Serious Economic Offences (later the Scorpions), the Public Protector and, notably, the Special Investigating Unit (SIU), chaired by Judge Willem Heath, which had the power to reverse any deal shown to have been corrupt.

This proposal drew the wrath of the cabinet, represented by Jeff Radebe, Trevor Manuel, Alec Erwin and Mosiuoa Lekota. They held a joint press conference and slammed the Auditor-General and Scopa for daring to criticise the cabinet and for insinuating that the cabinet could be involved in corruption. Thabo Mbeki himself poured scorn on Judge Willem Heath, calling into question the motives of the proposed investigation.

In another step to stop the investigation, the ANC's governance committee blasted its representatives on Scopa. Essop Pahad called the reports alleging massive corruption in the arms deal 'a litany of lies'. Andrew Feinstein in his book *After the Party* recalls Pahad asking him, 'Who do you think you are questioning the integrity of the government, the ministers and the president?'[4]

A series of events left any semblance of executive oversight in tatters. President Mbeki was ruthless in his defence of the arms deal. His contemptuous dismissal of Judge Heath on public television; the subsequent exclusion of the Heath Unit from any possible probe; the toxic letter addressed to Scopa under the name of Deputy President Jacob Zuma, but later proven to be from the pen of the president himself; the sacking of Andrew Feinstein as chairman of the ANC's Scopa study group and his subsequent resignation; the collapse of any resistance to the executive by ANC members of Scopa; the defiance of key ministers in their insistence that there was no corruption in the arms deal; the attempt (outvoted by the ANC majority) to move a motion of no confidence in Speaker Frene Ginwala because of her alleged partiality; the scorn poured on Gavin

Woods, the chairman of Scopa; all of this and more leave a very bad taste in the mouth and highlight the impotence of parliament when faced with so grave a question as corruption in high places.

Let it be quite clear, Scopa failed and parliament failed because of the ruthless exercise of power by President Thabo Mbeki and members of his cabinet. It was not merely the unnecessary purchase of sophisticated weapons, but the corruption which accompanied the entire sordid deal, that needed to be thoroughly investigated. This was a display of dominant politics reminiscent of the attitude and behaviour of the National Party when it held an overwhelming majority in parliament. There were very few heroes during this period. Those who did fight for parliament's integrity, like Gavin Woods, Andrew Feinstein, Patricia de Lille and Raenette Taljaard, are no longer in parliament and the assembly is the poorer for their departure.

Despite all the attempts by the ANC government to bury the arms deal, it has simply refused to go away. Largely due to the courageous determination of anti-arms campaigner Terry Crawford-Browne, in 2013 President Zuma announced a new commission of inquiry. It is to Zuma's credit that this inquiry is judicial in nature (though he announced it at the last possible minute before the Constitutional Court was due to find on Crawford-Browne's case, thus avoiding a much more dangerous situation), but already there have been a number of resignations. It will take many years for the commission to fulfil its mandate and it is difficult to be sanguine about the final outcome.

*   *   *

There are numerous other examples of the ANC's determination to control parliament, and they do so not only by using their majority in parliament but from Luthuli House as well. The Democratic Alliance lists at least seven 'debates of public importance' which they requested during 2012 which were turned down by the speaker: South Africa's high youth unemployment; the text book crisis in Limpopo; strike action at Lonmin Mine leading to the death of mine workers; the state of education in the country; the Mdluli saga; the impact of labour legislation on job creation; Nkandlagate.

There are outstanding questions regarding President Zuma's response during question time in parliament concerning his residence in Nkandla. According to the president, he was still paying a bond on his mansion, but the deed document for the property shows that the Ingonyama Trust is the owner (the Trust, headed by King Goodwill Zwelithini, manages 32 per cent of all land in KwaZulu-Natal on behalf of the state for the benefit of all its occupants). We have not heard the last word about Nkandla and this may yet prove to be Zuma's Achilles' heel.

The Protection of State Information Bill (the so-called Secrecy Bill) has been subject to considerable debate for months and has been strongly criticised by opposition parties in parliament, civil society and the media. Whilst improvements to the draft bill have been made, it still contains some controversial clauses that aim to make it an offence to disclose or be in possession of classified state information.

In my interview with Ben Turok, I asked him why he had walked out of parliament when the bells rang for voting on the Secrecy Bill. He told me that it was a very difficult decision. 'I drove towards parliament very concerned as to what I would do. I didn't know what I was going to do until the last minute. Shall I vote for the Bill, shall I abstain? Then I got up and walked out. I could not vote for the Bill. I drove home with very mixed feelings and knew that I would be in trouble with the chief whip and my caucus.' And so it turned out. He faced five charges under the ANC code of conduct and later the matter was left in the hands of the chief whip.

Gloria Borman, an ANC MP from Durban, was also torn as to what she should do regarding the Secrecy Bill. Gloria is a woman with strong Christian convictions and was unhappy with the Bill on both political and religious grounds. 'I did not know what I should do until the very last minute and then decided to abstain. My party was very angry, particularly about my speaking to the media as to why I had abstained. I was sent to Coventry, none of my colleagues would speak with me or be seen with me.'

Borman, like Turok, faced five charges and her case was also referred to the chief whip. The matter was taken no further. Disillusioned with widespread corruption, internal divisions and the lack of leadership, she expressed her dismay at the present state of the party. She is puzzled that although many in the leadership seem to be aware of the ills facing the party, they seem incapable of fixing what has gone wrong. She is concerned that parliament is not fulfilling its rightful role and in many ways is a 'lame duck'. She added, however, that the Ethics Committee and several other committees in parliament are doing good work. She has no intention of leaving the ANC and wants to be part of the reform of parliament.

Unfortunately, when the Secrecy Bill was voted on in its final stages, both Turok and Borman voted in favour of the bill. 'It is clear that the Parliamentary process has run its full course and that the relevant committees are exhausted. I therefore feel it is time for others to take up the debate, and rely on the good judgment of our top lawyers to decide,' Turok said to the *Mail & Guardian*, referring to his conviction that the bill would go to the Constitutional Court.[5]

* * *

Does the intolerance reflected by the ANC in its style of government hark back to the same brand of intolerance in the ANC leadership in exile? It is certainly clear that the ANC today has contempt for opposition of any kind. Democracy, according to Zuma at least, means the dominance of the majority rather than the protection of minorities.

When I interviewed Ronnie Kasrils on 22 September 2012, we had a wide-ranging discussion. He made several important points. First, there were many in exile who were not in favour of negotiations and were very suspicious of any move in this direction. He, together with Chris Hani, Joe Modise and Mac Maharaj, continued to pursue the armed struggle with renewed energy. Kasrils and others were not only suspicious of De Klerk and his party, but felt that they were not ready for negotiations. However, when this became a reality, they had to learn 'on the run'.

Second, he pointed out that a commitment to a one-party state was not only supported by the ANC in exile, but also by many inside South Africa. In particular, he referred to Blade Nzimande, minister of higher education, with his background in the union movement and the SACP. In

Kasrils' view, Nzimande is Stalinist in his views and contemptuous of all opposition to the ANC inside and outside of parliament. Nzimande, according to Kasrils, is particularly venomous in his attitude towards the media and very defensive of Zuma. Third, Kasrils is deeply disturbed at the corruption, the inefficiency, the maladministration and the rigidly centralised control in the party. Fourth, he is worried about Jacob Zuma, whom he described as 'cruel and uncaring'. He believes that Zuma's previous links with the intelligence department of the ANC and his current close relationship with all intelligence agencies make him a very powerful president who can use his access to information to keep his opponents within the party in check.

Kasrils concedes that when he was in exile, his first commitment was to MK and the armed struggle. Pluralism, a Bill of Rights, the division of powers, the role of parliament – these were the province of the intellectuals and academics like Mbeki, Albie Sachs and Kader Asmal. MK was not interested in human rights; its main object was the seizure of power by force of arms. He admits that a negotiated settlement proved to be the wisest course to follow, and appreciates the importance of the separation of powers, but speaks of his frustration with Luthuli House when he was a minister in parliament. He supports major reform in parliamentary procedure instead of majoritarianism, but fears that control is a *sine qua non* for the ANC.

Despite his severe criticism of the ANC, he still supports the party. When I asked him, 'What will happen if the ANC should lose at the polls?' his reply was, 'It will never happen.' I am not sure whether he meant that the ANC would never lose a national election, or that they would never relinquish power at any time! He did not elaborate on this key question.

It is my view, based on the record of the ANC in exile and in government, with their passion for control, their intolerance of opposition, and their stated belief that they are destined to rule 'until Jesus comes', that should they lose their majority they will refuse to accept the will of the people.

CHAPTER FOUR

People's Parliament

Parliament's strategic vision is to build an effective people's parliament that is responsive to the needs of the people, and that is driven by the ideal of realising a better quality of life for all the people of South Africa, and its mission is to represent and act as a voice of the people in fulfilling parliament's constitutional functions of passing laws and overseeing executive action.

— TASK TEAM ON OVERSIGHT AND ACCOUNTABILITY[1]

The above quotation focusing on the vision and mission for parliament is taken from a parliamentary report on oversight and accountability written in 2009. It is a powerful statement and if it were to be realised and put into practice, it would transform the current parliament. Regrettably, in 2014 this dream of a people's parliament has yet to come into effect.

It will be instructive to consider this report in some detail. It was written 15 years after the new parliament came into being, by the task team made up of representatives from all the parties in parliament. These are not voices from outside; these are the thoughts, the views, the mission of parliamentarians setting out certain mechanisms to guide the work of parliament in order to fulfil its vision and mission.

The report acknowledges that in the first decade of our new democracy the emphasis was on the transformation of South Africa's legislative landscape, and parliament's oversight function received less attention. Clearly, the aim of this parliamentary task team was to get a better balance, focusing not only on legislation, but also on oversight of the executive: 'The mandate of parliament is achieved through passing legislation, overseeing government action and facilitating public participation and international participation' (p 1).

The report emphasises that oversight ought not to be the role of the opposition only, but should be the role of the legislature as an institution. The team (it is important to remember that members of the ANC and opposition parties are the authors of this report) adopted the following definition of oversight: 'In the South African context, oversight is a constitutionally mandated function of legislative organs of state to scrutinise and oversee executive action and any organ of state'. Parliament has the power to 'conduct oversight of all organs of state including those at provincial and local government level', and 'The appropriate mechanism for parliament to conduct oversight of these organs of state would be through parliamentary committees' (p 4).

Important aspects of the oversight function include the following. First, 'oversight includes parliament's responsibility to detect and prevent abuse, arbitrary behaviour or illegal or unconstitutional conduct on the part of the government and public agencies. At the core of this function is the protection of the rights and liberties of citizens' (p 4). However, as we have seen in the previous chapter, abuse by government in using its overwhelming majority to promote the interests of the ANC or condone misdeeds by its leaders has not been checked by parliament, which has thus failed to protect the rights and liberties of the country's citizens. This is a vision yet to be realised.

The second function of oversight is in respect of how taxpayers' money is used. For the sake of transparency and efficiency, parliament ought to be the watchdog that calls the departments of government to account for their expenditure. Once again, this is an admirable vision and ought to be part of parliament's mission, but if one looks back at the long and heated debate on the arms deal (in which Scopa worked perfectly until ANC leadership interfered), it is clear that parliament has failed in this part of its mission.

A third oversight function is to ensure that 'policies announced by government and authorised by parliament are actually delivered' (p 5). One of the major deficiencies of government is the lack of delivery of essential services in many parts of the country. Every day it is reported that schools are dysfunctional, text books have not arrived, buildings are inadequate and toilet facilities non-existent. We read in the media of hundreds and thousands of people still living in squalid conditions. Delivery protests are the order of the day. So yet again, tragically, while the intention may be good, parliament has failed to ensure that policies so often glibly announced by government ministers are in fact carried out.

The final function of oversight in terms of the task team's report is 'to improve the transparency of government operations and enhance public trust in the government which is itself a condition of effective policy delivery' (p 5). Reference was made in the previous chapter to the so-called Secrecy Bill, which appeared to have been written with the concealment of the state's weaknesses in mind, threatening prison sentences for whistle-blowers and incautious journalists. On 26 April 2013, it was passed by a large majority in a joint session of parliament. The vote was 190 members in favour of the bill, with 75 against it. There was one abstention and 160 members were not there to vote.

This debate has been ongoing not only for months but for years, and many improvements have been made to the initial bill. However, there are many opposition members of parliament and members of civil society who believe that it is still flawed, and who join Ben Turok in hoping the Constitutional Court will do what parliament could or would not.

The bill was been sent to President Zuma in October 2013 for him to sign into law. However, he does have an alternative: the president could send the bill to the Constitutional Court for review before he actually signs it into law. This option was strongly recommended in the debate by opposition members of parliament. They were supported by many in civil society, including the Anglican Archbishop of Cape Town and the Catholic Bishops' Conference.

Moloto Mothapo, the ANC's parliamentary spokesman, offered a spirited defence of the bill.[2] He was particularly harsh on columnist Mondli Makhanya, who had written in a *Sunday Times* leading article (28 April 2013) that the 'ANC flock of loyal sheep bleats on cue in parliament', charging that ANC MPs had 'only a passing acquaintance with the contents of the bill and simply obeyed party instructions to press the green button'.

Mothapo declared that ANC MPs had spent countless hours debating the bill 'at various caucus meetings, led discussions at ANC branches and also educated constituencies they represent across South Africa on its contents'. The fact that there were more than 900 changes to the original bill, he said, suggested that the ANC had listened carefully to criticism from opposition benches, civil society and community interest groups. This, he claimed, was 'illustrative of a democratic organisation that listens to the views of others and is open to persuasion from even those it disagrees with'. He was emphatic that the bill was a good one, in line with the country's constitution, and that it strives to 'balance the classification of sensitive information in the interests of national security', as is happening in established democracies elsewhere in the world.

Professor Pierre de Vos, who teaches constitutional law at the University of Cape Town, sees the bill very differently. He acknowledges that 'The latest version, while still a thoroughly bad piece of legislation aimed at allowing the covering up of wrongdoings and abuse of power by the intelligence services, is much improved.' But he is of the opinion that the bill is unlikely to pass constitutional muster, for instance, referring to the powers of the minister of state security to authorise other bodies to classify information.

De Vos also believes that 'information' is too broadly defined and could include 'verbal announcements'. He suggests that verbal communication between the notorious Gupta family and the president could potentially be classified information. This may be stretching things a little too far. Is he seeing spooks where they don't exist? More seriously, De Vos argues that the Secrecy Bill allows a range of people and organs of state to 'censor information in the name of protecting national security' and adds, ominously, 'thus potentially imposing drastic limits on the right to freedom of expression and the right of access to information'. De Vos claims that as it stands, the bill would discourage investigative journalists and whistle-blowers who would be fearful of being sent to jail for up to 25 years if they inadvertently used information which was classified.

So there we have it. The official opposition, media in general, serious academics and many within civil society remain critical of the bill and are of the view that it will seriously impair freedom of expression. On the other hand, the ANC points to the vast improvements made to the original bill, maintains that the security of the state is critical and that the bill in no way limits natural debate and critique of government policy. Who is correct?

Whatever else is true, and whether or not Zuma refers the bill to the Constitutional Court, it will end up there eventually. Then we will have certainty as to whether the bill legitimately seeks to safeguard the security of the state or whether it is a draconian measure to cover up the abuse of power by the state. In a surprise move, Zuma, on 12 September 2013, instructed parliament to review 'unconstitutional' sections of the bill. He said that he had sent the bill back to parliament because of problems with two sections that 'lacked meaning and coherence' and were 'irrational'. The sections in question (sections 42 and 45) deal with the prosecution of people who deliberately hide government wrongdoing and corruption. Zuma should be congratulated on taking this step, but he could not afford to have the Constitutional Court reject the bill as unconstitutional.

One thing is clear: a great deal of the criticism of the bill arises from a deep mistrust of government and this in itself is a tragic commentary on the yawning gap between government and the people.

*   *   *

Having discussed the functions of oversight, the parliamentary task team's report offers a definition of accountability. In plain language, 'Accountability is the hallmark of modern democratic governance ... and if those in power cannot be held accountable in public for their acts or omissions, for their decisions, their expenditure or policies, then democracy is a mere cliché.' Accountability is far more than matters relating to finance: 'It has become a symbol of good governance both in the public and private sectors' (p 5). The report then proceeds to list the functions of accountability, all of which are worthy of commendation, including 'to enhance the integrity of public governance in order to safeguard government against corruption, nepotism, abuse of power and other forms of inappropriate behaviour'.

It is extraordinary that a parliamentary task team can write in such strong language – and yet South Africa seems to be riddled with corruption, almost from the top to the bottom of government. Nepotism is found everywhere. If you are a friend of the government, if you are a strong

63

and loyal supporter of the government, if you have family links with the government, your chances of securing a good position in either the public or the private sector are so much better. The report is excellent but sadly, given the number of times that misuse and the abuse of power are referred to, it has simply not been implemented.

A further aspect of the task team's vision and sense of mission is contained in a paragraph on page 6: 'In conducting oversight and accountability, the principles of cooperative government and intergovernmental relations must be taken into consideration, including the *separation of powers* and the need for all spheres of government and all organs of state to exercise their powers and perform their functions in a manner that does not encroach on the geographic, functional or institutional integrity of government in another sphere.' This endorsement of the separation of powers is in contradiction to the behaviour of government. The executive seems to be synonymous with Luthuli House and the influence of the tripartite alliance totally blurs the separation of power.

It is difficult to comprehend that government members of the task team actually agreed to and endorsed this report. I repeat, this is not a report by opposition members of parliament; a parliamentary task team put this together and I can only assume that the members of government who participated were either stating their personal preferences, knowing that they would be extremely difficult to fulfil, or were cynical and simply mouthed worthy concepts and a commitment to something which they really didn't believe would ever come about. The ANC with its large majority could still make the vision come true, but it lacks the will to implement the fine-sounding phrases.

The task team reminds parliament that 'Committees can interact with civil society organisations, organised business, experts and professional bodies as a way of enhancing accountability and can call ministers and departmental heads to account on any issue relating to any matter over which they are effecting accountability within the ambit of the provisions of Section 56.' The Constitution, section 56(2) states, 'The National Assembly must provide for mechanisms (a) to ensure that all executive organs of state in the national sphere of government are accountable to it; and (b) to maintain oversight of (i) the exercise of national executive authority including the implementation of legislation and (ii) any organ of state.'

The task team emphasises the importance of putting questions to the executive and sees this as one of the ways in which parliament holds the executive to account. It states that these questions can be posed for oral or written reply to the president, the deputy president or cabinet ministers. Clearly, this is an important part of parliament's business, but on page 32 of the report, having stated that it is generally assumed that a question will be answered within 14 days, the task team continues, 'It is still a moot point as to what happens to a question standing over more than once as there are such instances and no sanctions in this regard exist.'

The report was tabled in 2009, and yet in 2014 there are still serious complaints from opposition members that questions are either not answered at all, or take far too long to be answered. It seems that the speaker now decides which questions deserve to be answered. Ironically, in May 2013, a new 'Protocol for good practice and conduct' was distributed by the ANC to its whips. It urges members of parliament not to be too aggressive when questioning ministers: 'Questions should never be used to embarrass or ridicule ANC deployees.' The protocol further proposes that MPs who fail to abide by the rules of the caucus should face serious censure, including the loss of travel privileges, being blocked from promotion, being dismissed from committees, having fines imposed or even being kicked out of parliament.[3] This can only add to the docility of the majority of ANC MPs, to the detriment of executive oversight.

At the very beginning of the task team's report, it states that, 'The legislative and oversight programme of parliament demands capacity, competence and collective action.' Towards the end of the report, there is a long and interesting section on training. 'Training should take place based on the Constitution, rules and relevant practices in Parliament, as well as the public representative role of members to conduct oversight and pass legislation.' It is worth stressing that the task team's report in terms of training underlines that 'Members' training should incorporate a number of core competencies *affirming the understanding of the Constitution.*'

It is an admirable recommendation: clearly training and discipline are in short supply in parliament in current times. One wonders how many members of parliament have actually studied the Constitution and understand

and appreciate the responsibilities of parliament, particularly in terms of oversight of the executive. But the fact that the report notes that training is required and should be focused on the Constitution deserves praise and credit. It is to be hoped that such training will begin to bear fruit.

In the conclusion to the report, the task force states, 'The true test of democracy is considered the extent to which parliament can ensure that government remains accountable to the people by maintaining oversight of government's action. Whether parliament is indeed successful in effectively holding the executive accountable will ultimately depend on the extent to which committees and individual members of parliament actively exercise their oversight role.' Once again, this statement cannot be faulted; nor indeed can the following statement, 'Two critical factors for ensuring the success of this oversight model are firstly, the need to integrate parliament's public participation function with its overall oversight mechanism and, secondly, to provide the appropriate capacity, especially human resources, to committees and members for its execution. It is vital that all public participation processes become inputs to the work of appropriate committees.'

Having considered the implications of the task team's vision and mission for parliament, one can only recommend in the strongest terms that this report be reissued and made compulsory reading for every member of parliament. Unfortunately, it would appear that the task team's report is gathering dust on the shelves of parliament and is not being put into practice. There is no guarantee that if the report were dusted off and revisited, it would make any difference – until such time as the ANC no longer has a formidable majority. This is shameful, because there is much in this report to be strongly and warmly commended in terms of parliament being not just a rubber stamp, but becoming a true legislature.

*   *   *

What changes should take place to make parliament truly a 'people's parliament' as visualised by the task team? The mission and the vision is for a 'people's parliament' – but we have also seen that thus far the vision has not seen the light of day. So what needs to happen?

First, though the make-up of the national assembly is encouraging, it can also fill one with dismay. On the one hand, there is a diversity which the old white parliament never enjoyed. But on the other hand, the empty benches reveal that many members of parliament simply do not show up for debates. The salary of a parliamentarian is not inconsiderable and one would hope that at the very least MPs would be in regular attendance. The chief whip of the ANC has in recent times threatened to take action against ANC MPs who are absent from parliament without permission. Hopefully this will have a salutary effect on attendance. Further, it is distressing to note the very high turnover of members of parliament, particularly from the ANC ranks. This doubtless indicates the superior attractions of business.

Second, there ought to be at least a degree of competence within parliamentary representation. It appears that many who are appointed through the list system have minimal qualifications, and this shows in the lack of participation in debates and committee work by many MPs. It is legitimate to wonder whether the majority of MPs actually read and understand the content of legislation, and in particular the consequences which flow from each piece of legislation should it become law. From my observations of the plenary sessions and the committees at work, there seems to be a small coterie of ANC MPs who are competent and qualified, who do participate. But they seem to do this on behalf of the majority of party members. This obtains not only in the assembly when it meets, but also in committees. Very often ANC members appointed to the committees take no part in the proceedings, if they show up at all; they simply demonstrate which side they are on by hurling abuse at the opposition during discussion on important and often divisive issues. This lack of constructive involvement reinforces the view that most government members are told what to do, namely not to rock the boat.

Third, I have already referred to putting questions to cabinet ministers, and there is no doubt that this is a very powerful weapon in the hands of the opposition. But if questions are not answered timeously and fully by cabinet ministers, then they lose a great deal of their effectiveness. It follows therefore that there ought to be sanctions against the president and his cabinet if they fail to honour their responsibility in terms of questions put to them by the opposition.

Most importantly, what needs to change is the attitude of the ruling party. The same intolerance and determination to control which was prevalent in the ANC in exile is still apparent in their attitude to parliament. They also seem to have little appreciation of the separation of power. The necessary tension between the executive, the legislature and the courts has collapsed. Further, it is difficult to assess the influence of the two other groups that make up the tripartite alliance. There can be very little doubt that when important pieces of legislation are discussed, particularly those affecting the economy, the SACP and Cosatu wield considerable influence. This means that parliament is not really independent, and certainly is not a 'parliament of the people' when it is controlled by the ANC and its alliance partners.

* * *

Despite the laudable vision and mission 'to build an effective people's parliament' and for parliament to 'represent and act as a voice of the people', there is no reference to the current electoral system, nor any mention of the report of the Electoral Task Team of January 2003. This 2003 report, which was rejected by cabinet, is not referred to by the task team or even included in their bibliography.

The ETT, as it became known, was chaired by Dr Frederik van Zyl Slabbert. In his book, *The Other Side of History*, he writes about his appointment and his disillusionment with the cabinet's response to the final report:

> In my experience as a factotum/facilitator, I had never felt so used, abused and insulted. It started off badly and ended worse. Chief Mangosuthu Buthelezi, in his capacity as minister of home affairs, approached me in early 2001 and said that the cabinet had unanimously agreed that I should chair the task team ... I waited one year for my letter of appointment. I finally made an appointment with Deputy President Jacob Zuma. I said to him that the situation was becoming totally ridiculous and untenable and I was no longer available.

Zuma responded, 'Good God no, you can't. We will look like Mugabe!' Slabbert replied, 'If I don't get a letter within two weeks, I am out.'[4]

Slabbert goes on to report that a year after he was approached, the ETT got off the ground. He discusses the raising of funds, the appointment of the task team members and concludes with this pointed remark, 'We then listened to representations from all the parties in parliament and finally I decided the whole exercise was a waste of time and money. It is quite clear to me that although the majority on the ETT proposed a multi-member constituency system, the government preferred the status quo.'[5]

Slabbert tabled the report with majority and minority recommendations as well as the proceedings of a two-day workshop organised by the ETT. He writes, 'Apparently Kader Asmal, when discussing the report in cabinet, said the proceedings of the workshop should not be contained in the report because they were only included "to make the report look bulky." A friend serving on the cabinet, not Buthelezi, told me the report was not read or studied by anyone that he could recall.'[6]

His final comment: 'All in all, a disgusting and eminently forgettable experience, except for the excellent contributions of some of my colleagues.'[7]

Slabbert was wrong about one thing. While it may have been 'a forgettable experience' for him, ever since the report was published in 2003 it has refused to go away. In books, articles, conferences and debates, reference is frequently made to the report and in particular to the majority recommendation regarding a shift from the list system to a combined list/constituency-based system, which would approximate to a people's parliament far more than the current system.

What, then, is the essence of the ETT's report, and how did it come about? The need for legislation for an electoral system arises from the Constitution. In 1993, the Interim Constitution of the Republic of South Africa (Act 200 of 1993) provided for the members of the national assembly and legislators of the nine new provinces to be elected in 1994 'by a universal adult franchise in accordance with a system of proportional representation'. However, the provisions of the final Constitution relating to an electoral system do not extend beyond the 1999 elections. The Constitution requires that an electoral system be introduced through the enactment of national legislation. Thus, there is at present no electoral system prescribed for the conduct of national and provincial elections which were scheduled for the second or third quarter of 2004. It was this that led the cabinet to appoint the ETT to draft legislation for an electoral system for 2004, although, the time factor being a real consideration, it was never going to be possible for the ETT to complete its task before that election.

The Team decided that they should be 'as open, accessible and transparent as possible'. They therefore organised a series of meetings of civil society and media representatives. However, the minister of home affairs made it quite clear that they were to engage political parties throughout their deliberations. Following this injunction, the ETT asked each party in parliament to appoint a liaison person to facilitate communication. They also arranged a two-day round table conference and asked each party to send not only their liaison representative, but another three delegates to attend the workshop.

It soon became apparent that there were two schools of thought in the ETT: those who believed that the current system should be retained unchanged and others who believed that a larger measure of constituency representation should be built into the voting system. Regrettably, no unanimity or consensus could be reached between these two points of view.

The report does, however, point out that there was considerable consensus and even unity of purpose on other critical issues. Firstly, that the core values and principles of the Constitution should be reflected in the electoral system; that the preoccupation with accountability should not jeopardise the values of fairness, inclusiveness and simplicity; that the current electoral system should not be replaced or radically altered, and that the current electoral system enjoys considerable support, has served South Africa well through two sets of national and provincial elections and has contributed greatly towards transitional stability.

The issue which clearly divided the two schools of thought was the question of accountability. A great deal of the discussion and debate centred on this matter. The majority on the task team saw the perceived lack of accountability as a major problem in the current system. This was raised not only by some political parties but by most of the media representatives and in many of the submissions by NGOs and other interested parties.

The majority acknowledged that in terms of percentages of respondents, 74 per cent were satisfied with the fairness and equality of the present electoral system and 81 per cent with its inclusiveness: 'In the matter of accountability, however, while 68% felt that the elections helped voters hold political parties accountable, only 60% felt that the system helped voters hold individual representatives accountable. This resulted in 71% feeling that the candidates should come from the area they represent, which was seen as a means of improving their individual accountability.'[8]

The majority recommendations were summed up in the following way: 'The nub of the majority view is that it is worthwhile to make legislative provision for an electoral system that can evolve towards a larger multi-membership constituency system with a compensatory national list. The majority feels that with the introduction of this constituency system, it does not mitigate against the core values of fairness, inclusiveness and simplicity characteristic of the current system.'[9]

It is important to note in particular that the majority report believed that 'to the extent that an electoral system can make some contribution towards political accountability, the majority is satisfied that the proposed electoral system will do so demonstrably and effectively'. In conclusion, 'If nothing else, this proposal, if accepted, will keep an essential debate alive on the ways and means by which political accountability can be strengthened in the South African democracy. That this is necessary and important was seen as common cause by all the parties, NGOs and media representatives with whom the ETT interacted.'[10]

The majority report was signed by Dr F Van Zyl Slabbert as chairperson, Mr Norman du Plessis, Prof Norman Jøgen Elklit, Prof Glenda Fick, Mr Nicholas Haysom, Dr Wilmot James, Adv Rufus Malatji and Ms Dren Nupen.

The minority report, signed by Mr Zam Titus, Mr Tefo Raditapole, Adv Pansy Tlakula and Mr SS van der Merwe, essentially supported the continuation of the list system, thus opposing the introduction of legislation calling for more direct constituency representation in parliament. They based their report on the final position adopted by the political parties represented in parliament, as follows: six parties with 307 representatives in the national assembly wanted the present system to be retained;

three parties with 74 representatives in the national assembly wanted some kind of multi-member constituency system with overall proportionality being restored by way of national party lists; and two parties with 17 representatives in the national assembly did not express firm preferences.

Further, the survey conducted by the ETT reflects that the majority of the public is in favour of the present system. The minority report acknowledges that there is a desire for more contact with parliamentary representatives but that this could be achieved by strengthening constituency offices and with the use of modern technology affording greater contact by MPs.

The minority report agreed with the basic values referred to above. First, as regards fairness: 'Every eligible voter should not only have the opportunity to vote but all votes as far as possible should be of equal value.' The report stressed that 'the current system is fully proportional, therefore represents the ultimate in fairness and thereby promotes the value of universal adult suffrage'. Second, inclusivity: 'Given the demographic, ethnic, racial and religious diversity of the South African society, our electoral system should allow the widest possible degree of participation of different political preferences in representative legislatures. The current system where even the smallest party can gain representation if it musters enough votes for a single seat, provides the ultimate in inclusivity.' Third, 'an electoral system that is complex would negatively impact on its fairness and inclusivity. The present system is simple enough to meet all the necessary criteria.'[11]

In sum, the crucial difference between the two reports is the question of accountability. As we have seen, the majority report proposed the introduction of direct constituency representation together with the list system, thereby guaranteeing proportionality, which they believed would result in greater accountability by parliament to voters. The minority report, on the other hand, did not deny the importance of accountability but was of the view that this could be achieved through regular elections. 'How do those who give a mandate through the vote call to account those who are supposed to perform in terms thereof? As far as an electoral system is concerned the answer is: at the next elections. At regular intervals, the voters can either revoke or renew the mandate they gave to a political party or a candidate.'[12]

The minority report emphasised why it could not support the majority report: 'Firstly, the very strong case made out for the retention of the present system in submissions to the ETT and at the conference. Secondly, our own conviction that the retention of the present system is essential to support reconciliation, nation building, peace, stability and good governance.' They concluded that, 'The present electoral system was introduced primarily to ensure the promotion of political diversity within our legislatures and broad political representation. These are not short-term proposals which can be attained overnight.' The minority report also concluded that, 'There is no ideal universal electoral system. Every system has its advantages and disadvantages. In South Africa we have a system that our electorate has bought into, that cannot be improved on for fairness and inclusivity, and which meets our current challenges as a country.'[13]

It is 10 years since the Electoral Task Team submitted its report concerning possible alterations to the electoral system in South Africa. But reverberations surrounding that report continue, both inside and outside parliament. On 4 March 2013, the Democratic Alliance tabled a bill entitled 'Electoral Amendment Bill (a proposed section 75 bill)'. In the objects of the bill, it states:

> The electoral system for the National Assembly that operates in South Africa (and which was entrenched in the Constitution until after the 1999 election) is one in which voters vote for political parties, and each party gets that share of the seats in the National Assembly reflecting as closely as possible the proportion of votes that party obtained in the election. The result is an equitable translation of votes in to seats, and therefore equitable representation for all political parties. The advantages of this system is that it is inclusive, it is immune to gerrymandering, it is perceived to be fair, and although not as understandable as a single-member constituency system, it is simple enough to be widely understood. However, the major weaknesses of the [current] system are the lack of accountability of members of the National Assembly to individual voters or identifiable groups of voters who elected them. This in turn leads to alienation by voters from the political system. There is currently no direct link between the voting public and

individual MPs. There is merely a link between the public and political parties. In practice, this means that the voters do not have 'ownership' of members of the National Assembly... The arbitrary allocation by political parties of MPs to non-existent 'constituencies' is a very poor substitute, as there is not accountability to, nor mandate from, the voters in those constituencies. Finally, MPs are often unable to perform constituency duties effectively since they enjoy no particular status or standing in the 'constituencies' to which they are allocated.

The bill differs in some detail from the Slabbert report but it is an unequivocal endorsement of the majority that called for constituency representation so that voters could have a greater say in who represented them in parliament and therefore be better placed to call parliamentarians to account. As James Selfe, chair of the DA's federal executive, stated at a press conference on 4 March 2013, 'People have no way of voting out an MP who does not perform ... In a list PR system, there is no geographical linkage between MPs and voters. The allocation by political parties of MPs to non-existent "constituencies" is a very poor substitute, as there is not accountability to, nor mandate from, the voters in those constituencies.' This is certainly a step in the right direction, but it is highly unlikely that it will ever be debated in parliament. More's the pity.

There have also been voices raised outside parliament. For example, Paul Hoffman SC, the director of the Institute for Accountability in Southern Africa, called for a referendum on the current electoral system. He states that he has formally asked President Jacob Zuma to call a referendum on the matter.[14] It is a long shot and I can't imagine that the president will accede to this request. Zuma certainly has been silent on the matter since the request was sent to him.

Another major South African voice that has entered the debate is that of Mamphela Ramphele. She acknowledges that proportional representation was correctly chosen to ensure that minority parties had a presence in parliament. However, in her view, 'Part of the problem arises from the electoral clause which was meant to be a sunset clause but remains in our Constitution unamended.'[15] She makes the very bold promise that her citizens' movement will '... galvanise the voices of citizens around this issue and make it impossible for any one of the parties or individuals standing for parliament in 2014 to do so without having made a commitment to changing that electoral clause'. She writes and speaks with great urgency and passion on the matter, but it seems a very big ask. Persuading all parties to commit themselves to changing the electoral clause by 2014 is going to take a great deal more than that.

There are a number of other NGOs who are on record asking for direct constituency representation. One small NGO, My Vote Counts, has entitled its campaign exactly that, the objective being 'to improve the transparency and inclusiveness of elections in South Africa to give us all a stronger voice'. This organisation argues for the electoral system to be changed so that people have a say in electing individual MPs from their constituencies. It acknowledges that proportional representation has much to commend it and should remain, but that at least 50 per cent of the members of parliament should be elected directly by constituencies.

It is encouraging that there is a clamour for direct representation by voters instead of leaving it in the hands of the party bosses. But it is clear that no attempt, however passionate or aggressive, will enable the changes to be made in time for the 2014 election. The best one can aim for is to put pressure on the government to appoint a new commission to review the Electoral Task Team report and to consider enabling greater participation by voters in the election of members of parliament. They could do this by debating the DA's electoral reform bill. Unfortunately, it is true that the list system is very seductive and there may well be other parties in parliament who will also continue to subscribe to this system because it gives them control over their organisations.

The major problem, therefore, is a lack of desire by the ruling party to be truly accountable and a determination to control its parliamentary representatives – both those who currently occupy their seats in parliament and those who will be there after the next election.

The previous all-white parliament was unrepresentative and devalued as a consequence. However, there was one positive feature: MPs were elected by constituencies and this brought the voters much closer to parliament. It was tragic and deplorable that the former parliamentary system excluded the vast majority of South Africans, but the emphasis on constituency-based elections for those who could vote should inform us today when parliament is finally representative of all South Africans. As the majority report of the ETT put it, 'Putting a face to politicians seems to be the only way to increase accountability significantly ... the current system makes no contribution to this' (p 24).

*   *   *

In summary, parliament is too important an institution to write off as merely a rubber stamp or a lame duck. Despite its inaction and poor decision-making, it does afford a very valuable opportunity for opposition parties to criticise and offer alternative policies and positions. This in turn enables the media to report on the proceedings so that the public is informed. It is also true that the committee system has greatly improved the tenor of the debates. Even ANC members have been known to call department heads appearing before the various committees to account.

Parliament must be recognised as the key legislator with specific duties to oversee the executive. That it does not always measure up is no reason to ignore, dismiss or abandon it as a key part of the separation of powers. Opposition parties, the media and civil society must continue to strive to bring about a true people's parliament, responsive to the needs of all the people of South Africa. The ANC must not be allowed to use parliament to advance the party at their expense.

CHAPTER FIVE

The Role of the Judiciary in a Failing State

*This constitution is the supreme law of the Republic; law or conduct
inconsistent with it is invalid and the obligations imposed by it must be fulfilled.*
— CONSTITUTION OF THE REPUBLIC OF SOUTH AFRICA, 1996, CHAPTER I(2)

In the preamble, the objectives of the Constitution are clearly spelled out –

Heal the divisions of the past and establish a society based on democratic values, social justice and fundamental human rights;

Lay the foundations for a democratic and open society in which government is based on the will of the people and every citizen is equally protected by law;

Improve the quality of life of all citizens and free the potential of each person; and

Build a united and democratic South Africa able to take its rightful place as a sovereign state in the family of nations.

The preamble, with echoes of the Freedom Charter, is a clarion call to all South Africans and in particular the elected government, to commit to a constitutional democracy which will bring far-reaching results in its wake. The healing of the nation is not only dealing with the past, important as this is; it is also the building of a future which is based on social justice and human rights. This is part of the genius of our Constitution; it acknowledges the past but is oriented towards the future. The Constitution explicitly acknowledges that there is still work to be done to realise a true democracy.

The preamble envisages a political system which is based on the will of the people and a government that is committed to the rule of law giving protection to every citizen, and offers the daring vista where the improvement of the quality of life for each person will be a reality and not an empty promise.

Finally, the preamble stresses the need for unity in South Africa based on democratic principles acceptable to all. This is a tough ask of any new government assuming office. It is particularly demanding, bearing in mind the horrific legacy of 300 years of colonialism and a system of racial discrimination which reached into every area of life, its obscene and demeaning tentacles squeezing the life chances of more than 80 per cent of the population. It is also a seemingly impossible list of goals to demand of a new government, whose leadership has either been incarcerated in prison or in exile and/or living fearfully, many underground – thus, a president and a cabinet and MPs and provincial leaders assuming responsibility after being routinely and legally excluded from experience in government at every level.

Nevertheless, the preamble was endorsed by Mandela and the ANC, and the current government must be challenged on that endorsement whenever or wherever it fails to live up to the inspiring objectives of the preamble. And this is what is absolutely new in South African politics: the Constitution, not parliament, is sovereign. No longer can a majority government ride roughshod over human rights by passing laws over which the courts have no say.

For months I tried to arrange an appointment with the speaker of the national assembly. I wanted to ask him what it meant that the Constitution and not parliament was sovereign. Finally I was told to be at his office at 2.00 pm on 5 June 2013. I left home in good time but got caught up in a traffic jam and became more and more anxious about being on time. I arrived in his plush office with a minute to spare. I was sweating and could hardly concentrate; luckily I had a dictaphone to record the interview. However, before I could ask my first question, the speaker launched into a lecture on the differences between the old and new parliaments:

The old parliament was supreme and no court of law could change anything. This is the big difference. In the new dispensation, the Constitution is supreme and all the laws that we make should be in line with the Constitution. The Constitution is the supreme law of the land so any law that we make must be in line with the Constitution and this means that parliament itself is no longer supreme. There will inevitably be tension but this is what we as South Africans wanted and that is why we elected a new democratic dispensation where all are subject to the rule of law, to the constitutional rule.

He was right. The differences were profound, not only in terms of the superiority of the Constitution in relation to the legislature. A few months earlier, I had visited parliament for the first time since I had walked out in 1986. Memories flooded back. I recalled the first day I attended the House of Assembly in 1974 and had mixed feelings of nostalgia and relief. Sitting in the gallery, I was delighted to witness a fully representative parliament. I was also relieved that Vorster and PW Botha were ghosts of the past and I didn't have to face them ever again.

*   *   *

The late Arthur Chaskalson, in an address to the Cape Law Society on 9 November 2012, made the point of the Constitution's sovereignty very powerfully. 'The supremacy of the Constitution and the rule of law require everybody in our country, including parliament and the executive, to obey the law and to respect and uphold the provisions of the Constitution. Our Constitution is explicit about this obligation, and the courts are mandated to be the guardian of the Constitution.'

Chaskalson stressed that 'courts are told that they must declare legislation or conduct that is inconsistent with the Constitution to be invalid'. He emphasised the difference between the former regime and today when he stated, 'This obligation of courts is in stark contrast to the role of the courts when legislative supremacy prevailed. This can be described by referring to a passage from a 1934 judgment of the appellate division, then our highest court, where the chief justice of that time said, "Parliament may make any encroachment it chooses upon the life, liberty or property of any individual subject to its sway … and it is the function of the courts of law to enforce its will."'

Justice Laurie Ackermann was appointed by then President Nelson Mandela as a judge on the Constitutional Court, where he served for 10 years. Earlier Ackermann had resigned from the bench. When I asked him in an interview on 6 June 2013 why he had done so, he replied, 'One of the major reasons that I resigned in 1987 from the bench is that I felt the way apartheid was being enforced and the emergency laws was destroying the law and there was very little one could do on the bench to use cracks and crevices to do justice. Every time there was a judgment in favour of liberty, the statute would be amended and the door would close and one had an oath of office and you couldn't pretend that you were enforcing some other system of law. There was parliamentary sovereignty; you couldn't interpret that away and I think the administration of justice was becoming very difficult to reconcile with one's concept of justice and therefore decided that I had no alternative but to resign.'

In this statement, Ackermann underlined exactly how radical the shift from parliamentary sovereignty to constitutional democracy was; now, the Constitution is supreme and therefore not only parliament but also the executive are answerable to it.

Max Sisulu drives home the sovereignty of the Constitution: 'Significantly, even though the new parliament is democratically elected and representative, it is no longer supreme. In *Speaker of the National Assembly vs De Lille*, it was held that the Constitution "is the ultimate source of all lawful authority in the country. No parliament, however bona fide or eminent its membership, no president, how formidable be his reputation or scholarship, and no official, however efficient or well-meaning, can make any law or perform any act which is not sanctioned by the Constitution."'

In section 165(2) and following, the Constitution provides that courts are independent, subject only to the law and the Constitution which they must apply impartially without fear, favour or prejudice and that no person or organ of state may interfere with the functioning of the courts (section 165(3)). Furthermore, in section 6 of Schedule 2 to the Constitution, the oath of the office of judges requires them to swear or affirm that they will uphold and protect the Constitution and the human rights entrenched in it and will administer justice to all persons alike without fear or favour or prejudice in accordance with the Constitution and the law. Chaskalson, in his address to the Cape Town Law Society referred to above, put it succinctly: 'It is essential and indispensable for the discharge of its duties and the exercise of the powers vested in it that the judiciary should be and should be seen to be independent.'

However, the sovereignty of the Constitution and the independence of the judiciary must be seen in context with two other arms of government, namely the executive authority which is vested in the president, and the legislative authority which is vested in parliament. The Constitutional Court has held that the separation of powers could provide checks and balances to ensure accountability. Sisulu refers to the case *Doctors for Life International vs the Speaker of the National Assembly*. In its decision, the Constitutional Court emphasised that the Constitution afforded parliament a very wide discretion to determine its internal procedures and processes. The Court stressed that only the Constitutional Court could inquire whether parliament fulfilled a constitutional obligation. Sisulu quotes further from the judgment: 'The Court pointed out that section 167(4) of the Constitution conferred exclusive jurisdiction on the Constitutional Court in a number of crucial political areas to preserve the comity between the judicial branch of government and the other branches of government by ensuring that only the highest court in constitutional matters intrudes into the domain of the other branches of government.'

Sisulu also reminds his readers that 'the Cape High Court twice cautioned members of parliament to preserve the independence of the court and not launch unfounded applications to court on parliamentary matters that could be resolved internally as this would lead to the politicisation of the judiciary.'[2] He refers to a statement made by Justice Dennis Davis: 'Drawing the judiciary into every and all political disputes as if there was no other forum to deal with the political impasse relating to policy ... into issues which are beyond their competence or intended jurisdiction or which have been deliberately or carefully constructed legally so as to ensure that the other arms of the state deal with these matters can only result in jeopardy for our constitutional democracy.'[3] Sisulu concludes by affirming that, 'While the three arms of government are independent, each arm must respect the functional independence of the other arms to ensure the preservation of our democracy.'[4]

Paul Holden, in *Who Rules South Africa?*, makes the point that the Constitutional Court is very aware of the inevitable tension between the three arms of government. He writes: 'This tension is arguably something to which the judiciary has often been alive, arguably leading to a more cautious jurisprudence than many social activists might desire.'[5] Furthering this point, with reference to three key cases which indicate the Constitutional Court's approach to justiciable socio-economic rights,[6] Holden maintains that the Constitutional Court had two choices. The first was that of the 'minimum core' approach, referring to a judgment articulated by the United Nations Committee on Economic, Social and Cultural Rights where it was argued 'that it was incumbent on all states who were party to the covenant to ensure that a basic minimum of socio-economic services were to be delivered to every citizen'. If the court had adopted this approach, 'it would have been profound; it would effectively have established itself as a potential governance monitor, prescribing that the government provided a basic level of socio-economic services to every person in the country'. This could 'be construed as a form of "intense judicial activism"'. And this is exactly what the Court did not want to do. It respected the separation of powers. Nevertheless, Holden points out that some activists and even legal experts were in favour of such an approach 'as it would act as a mechanism that provided a baseline of delivery against which the state could be measured. Without it, it was feared enforcement of the bill of rights would lack teeth.' Instead of adopting this 'minimum core' approach, the Constitutional Court developed a line of argument referred to as 'reasonableness'.

There are four important issues which, if not properly addressed, could reduce the effectiveness of the judiciary. Firstly, the administration of justice is a very worrying feature in terms of the prosecution authority under the present government. We have witnessed long delays in the appointment of key personnel, and often the persons who are finally appointed prove to be incompetent and have to be replaced. This, coupled with maladministration at almost all levels in our courts and in the police, gives little cause for confidence to the general public that they will have access to justice. According to a survey conducted by the Human Sciences Research Council in 2012, one in three South Africans believes the courts discriminate against poor black South Africans. The survey found a lack of public confidence in the criminal justice system. This is extremely disturbing and calls for an urgent reform of the system by the department of justice and constitutional development.

Ackermann, quoted earlier, stressed the need for urgent reform in the administration of justice when he remarked, 'What the lay public doesn't sufficiently realise is that the strength and the ability and the competence of the court depend to a significant extent upon the quality of the legal representatives, whether for the state or the individual, or private parties. The better your counsel, the better your judgment should be because you should have had on both sides the best arguments that could be made for the contending cases with full reasons and justification given by counsel and it is a very invidious task when you have one of the parties not properly or adequately represented.'

The second issue is that many people are denied access to our courts because they simply cannot afford the costs involved. In this respect, constitutional law expert Jackie Dugard is critical even of the Constitutional Court: in her view, the court has failed on two grounds: to lobby for legal representation for the poor in civil matters, and to provide direct access to the court for those with big problems but empty pockets. She has recommended that South Africa should consider the Costa Rican model, which accepts any direct claim in written form and considers about 17 000 cases each year. She continues, 'The Constitutional Court risks becoming an elite institution increasingly inaccessible to the poor.'[7]

In his address to the Cape Law Society on 9 November 2012, Chaskalson also refers to this matter of access to the courts for the very poor. He refers to the need for the legal profession to be absolutely independent –

> But there is a corresponding obligation that flows from this, and that is that the profession must conduct its affairs in a manner consistent with the public interest. The duties owed to clients to act without fear

or favour, to the court to act honourably and generally to observe high professional standards are important parts of the profession's responsibility to the public. However, that is not all; the public must have access to the profession which would have no right to assert that it serves the public interest if it were to serve only the elite in our society. What is important is that legal services should be available to all who need them and in particular to those who look to the profession as an institution that will uphold and protect the rights of everyone and not only the rich.

The fact that Chaskalson was for many years head of the Legal Resources Centre, an institution which continues to give legal assistance to those who cannot afford it, lends this statement particular credibility.

A third critical issue which can either hinder or assist the courts is the appointment of judges. Whilst the Constitution is sovereign and the Constitutional Court could be seen as more equal than the executive and the judiciary, its powers are limited to the extent that judges of the Constitutional Court are appointed by the president, who in turn must take into account recommendations by the Judicial Services Commission (JSC). Because of the controversy surrounding this commission, it is worthwhile noting its full membership, which is found in section 178 of the Constitution:

> The chief justice, who presides at meetings of the commission; the president of the supreme court of appeal; one judge president designated by the judges president; the cabinet member responsible for the administration of justice or an alternate designed by that cabinet member; two practising advocates nominated from within the advocates' profession to represent the profession as a whole, and appointed by the president; two practising attorneys nominated from within the attorneys' profession to represent the profession as a whole, and appointed by the president; one teacher of law designated by teachers of law at South African universities; six persons designated by the national assembly from among its members, at least three of whom must be members of opposition parties represented in the assembly; four permanent delegates to the national council of provinces designated

together by the council with the supporting vote of at least six provinces; four persons designated by the president as head of the national executive, after consulting the leaders of all parties in the national assembly; and, when considering matters relating to a specific high court, the judge president of that court and the premier of the province concerned or an alternate designated by each of them.

When comparing the Interim Constitution and the final Constitution, it is clear that in the latter the JSC is heavily weighted in favour of the legislature and the executive. This shift in representation is, in my view, one of the reasons that the JSC is a matter of acute controversy.

This is a very powerful list of members and their responsibility is critical to ensure the good administration of the Constitutional Court and other courts. This section, which deals with the membership, should be read in conjunction with section 174, which relates to the appointment of judicial officers: 174(1) states that 'Any appropriately qualified woman or man who is a fit and proper person may be appointed as a judicial officer.' 174(2) states that 'The need for the judiciary to reflect broadly the racial and gender composition of South Africa must be considered when judicial officers are appointed.' Both of these sub-clauses have to be taken seriously but it appears to some that the JSC has failed to hold the two in tension, not always adhering to the need for 'appropriately qualified persons'.

Ackermann has some very strong words on this failure to hold the two clauses in tension. 'With great respect, I think the JSC has not correctly understood and applied section 174 of the Constitution ... I think it is very clear: you can't appoint somebody unless a person is appropriately qualified and is a fit and proper person. It is very difficult to keep the tension, but it is vital. One would want the judiciary to reflect, in an ideal world, the gender and racial composition of society, but this does not say that that must happen in two or three years. I think mistakes have been made. I think people have been appointed who were not as yet fit and proper and who were not as yet qualified.' It is clear from the Constitution that judges should be fit and proper persons and qualified at the time of their appointment. Ackermann states emphatically, 'You can't appoint a potential.' He is particularly concerned about the process followed in the interviews which the JSC holds before coming to a decision on who they should recommend to the president. 'The questioning doesn't seem to be focused on the experience, the training, the legal ability, of the people concerned but solely on "What did you do before 1994?"' And I don't think that is the proper procedure to follow.'

I put it to him that this doesn't seem to be the reason for the non-appointment of someone as eminent as Adv Geoffrey Budlender, who had an impeccable human rights record before 1994 not only as a student but also as a lawyer, an advocate and an acting judge. Ackermann was nonplussed: 'The fact that Budlender had been working with the Legal Resources Centre, who were trying to use the law to the maximum of their ability to help the underdog, the disadvantaged, the discriminated against, whether it means they suspect him of having too independent a mind, I just don't understand. It doesn't make sense at all.' In my own view, the main reason was that they feared that Budlender, if appointed, would urge far greater emphasis on economic and social action.

Ackermann had additional comments. 'I have spoken to people who have been interviewed and they said that the most powerful impression that was created is that the minds of those doing the interviewing had been made up before the interview started and the interview was absolutely perfunctory. Really a farce. That is shameful and is not in accordance with the law.' He is also critical of the appointment of the chief justice. He refers to Justice Dikgang Moseneke, who was overlooked in this appointment. 'On all objective criteria he was obviously qualified, experienced, all the qualifications that you could possibly wish for: fully in the struggle at the age of 15, sentenced to 10 years on Robben Island. I don't want to bad-mouth the chief justice who has been appointed, but with great respect, he is so junior to Moseneke in his background and qualifications and experience that it is really not intelligible to me.' He might have added, '… other than that Zuma favoured him for reasons best known to Zuma'. That is certainly my view.

He is not alone in his concerns regarding the appointments made in recent times by the JSC. The Helen Suzman Foundation has decided to take the JSC to court and in a widely published statement issued on 7 June 2013, it states:

> The Helen Suzman Foundation (HSF) has launched legal action against the JSC in order to clarify the procedure and decision-making relating to the nomination of persons for judicial office. The HSF, in challenging the lawfulness of a particular process of the JSC, hopes to clarify and establish the correct interpretation and implementation of section 174 of the constitution. In a constitutional democracy an independent judiciary must be staffed by judges of the highest intellectual ability and moral character who not only understand but also live the spirit of the constitution. The HSF supports the constitutional imperatives of judicial transformation; however there is a growing perception that talented candidates for judicial appointment and advancement are being overlooked for reasons that are not clear or explicit.

The statement refers to comments made by the chief justice in his capacity as JSC's chairman and by its spokesman, Adv Dumisa Ntsebeza SC, as well as the resignation of Izak Smuts SC from the JSC. It continues, 'The purpose of our action thus is to ensure that the JSC's decision-making process is consistent with the provisions of the Constitution. Although the HSF is challenging the lawfulness of a particular set of facts, it is hoped that clarity will be obtained in respect of the JSC's methodology in nominating and selecting candidates for judicial office.'

It is clear that we have not heard the last word about the JSC and its nomination of judges. Whatever else is true, it would be a tragedy if the high standards set in the initial appointment of judges to the Constitutional Court in 1994 were in any way to be jeopardised by the appointment of persons lacking the experience or the training which should be a central part of a judge's place on the Constitutional Court.

It is right that every effort should be made to transform the judiciary. Chaskalson has pointed out that about 60 per cent of our judges are now black whereas in 1994, there were only three black judges.[8] Significant progress has been made, but it is imperative that merit on the one hand and transformation on the other should be held in tension.

A fourth issue, and perhaps the most serious in terms of being a threat to the independence of the judiciary, is the incessant criticism of the Constitutional Court by the ANC government. Paul Holden refers to a statement made by the secretary-general of the ANC, Gwede Mantashe, which gives us an indication of the strong and even hostile views of some of the ANC leadership towards the Constitutional Court. Mantashe made his statement after the Constitutional Court judges laid a complaint against Judge John Hlophe, who, it is alleged, sought to influence two judges into supporting Zuma in a pending appeal before the Court:

> This is psychological preparation of society so when the constitutional court judges pounce on our president, we should be ready at that point of time ... our revolution is in danger; we must declare to defend it to the very end ... you hit the head, you kill the snake. When there is an attack on him, it is a concerted attack on the head of the ANC. Everybody says it is an innocent attack on him. We will know it is an attack on the ANC.

This flies in the face of the repeated acknowledgement by the Constitutional Court that it accepts that the separation of powers must be adhered to. Deputy Chief Justice Dikgang Moseneke stated very clearly that 'Courts must refrain from entering the exclusive terrain of the executive and legislative branches of government unless the intrusion is mandated by the Constitution.'[9]

Despite the assurances given by the Constitutional Court regarding its appreciation of the separation of powers, the government is clearly unhappy at being outranked – and this means unhappy with the Constitution itself, from which the Constitutional Court derives its powers. This is highly dangerous and must be opposed by all who believe in a constitutional democracy.

It is understandable that the ANC feels aggrieved by a court that overturns some of the laws it seeks to put on the statute books. After more than 100 years of opposing the exclusivity of racial parliaments with sovereign powers that no court could challenge, at great expense, hardship, deprivation and loss of life, the ANC is the democratically elected government but is unable to have the final say concerning its policies! It must be galling for a party that had as its watchword the 'seizure of power' to have its powers fundamentally checked in this way. However, we must be very clear on this issue: this was a choice made during the negotiations. The ANC accepted the Interim Constitution on which South Africa's historic election was held in 1994. Furthermore, one of their leaders, Cyril Ramaphosa, chaired the constitutional commission, and the final Constitution was adopted by parliament, which included the vote of the ANC (it is interesting that Ramaphosa, recently elected as deputy president of the ANC, in 2013 urged young people in schools and colleges to accept the Constitution as 'their bible'!).

President Zuma demonstrated his intentions and his misunderstanding of what it means to have a constitutional democracy when he argued in a speech at the Access to Justice conference in Johannesburg in 2011, 'South Africa has to distinguish the areas of responsibility between the judiciary and the elected branches of government, especially with regard to government policy formulation.' He continued, 'The powers conferred on the courts cannot be superior to the powers resulting from the political, and consequently administrative, mandate resulting from popular democratic elections.' The Constitution, however, is clear and Zuma is dead wrong – as quoted at the beginning of the chapter, it is the supreme law.

It is clear that not only individuals but also political parties must adhere to and accept the superiority of the Constitution. The only recourse for the ANC is to obtain a two-thirds majority in the national assembly. It is imperative therefore that the voters in the 2014 election do not give the ANC the power to change the Constitution to suit themselves.

The ANC has enjoyed a large majority since South Africa's first democratic election in 1994. It is particularly important where one party has an overwhelming majority that there should be checks and balances. If the ANC does not want to be seen to be unconstitutional, it should adhere to the rule of law in its law-making, its appointment of senior personnel and its governance. But, as an Australian jurist, Murray Gleeson, put it, 'People who exercise political power and claim to represent the will of people do not like being checked or balanced.' The Constitution and the Constitutional Court are formidable opponents of any political party that seeks to abuse power. This is writ large on the canvas of South Africa's contemporary political arrangement and every effort to safeguard the Constitution and to uphold the independence of the Constitutional Court must be a priority for all those who believe in democracy and justice.

Edwin Cameron, a judge on the Constitutional Court, gave an illuminating and wise speech at the *Sunday Times* Literary Awards in 2013. In his speech, he reminded the ANC government – which from time to time is critical of the powers of the Constitution and indeed all those who seek to defend it – why there is reason to be cautiously optimistic concerning the period of South Africa's history under the Constitution adopted in 1996.

He offers five reasons for his optimism: first, though the Constitution has not yet stood the test of time, it is on its way to doing so, despite the disputes and turmoil which have sought to challenge its validity; second, the separation of powers has proven practically effective (I have given examples of this cooperation between the judiciary, the executive and the legislature, despite the criticism of some in government); third, the nature of constitutionalism is widely disseminated in South Africa; fourth, the judiciary is strong and honest (thus my argument above calling for merit and integrity to be the hallmarks of the appointment of all judges), and fifth, the fundamental structure and values of the Constitution uphold democracy, equality, a separation of powers between independent institutions and a commitment to social justice.

It is to be hoped that Cameron's timely reminder of the cardinal importance of the Constitution as our yardstick for good governance will be widely read. Hopefully it will also be a warning to those who would seek to undermine the Constitution and a call on government leaders and citizens alike to defend it with passionate and steadfast vigour.

But let us be on our guard. If the ANC cannot amend the Constitution there is another ominous approach which they could adopt: they could ensure that judges appointed to the Constitutional Court are reluctant to take a stand against the ANC. The findings of the Constitutional Court could alter dramatically. Again, this underlines the absolute need for people of experience, merit and integrity to be appointed to the Constitutional Court, and indeed, to all our courts.

CHAPTER SIX

Corruption in a Failing State

There can be no gainsaying that corruption threatens to fell at the knees virtually everything we hold dear and precious in our hard-won constitutional order.

— CONSTITUTIONAL COURT JUDGMENT [1]

If corruption were an event in the Olympic Games, the ANC government would be festooned with silver and bronze – and perhaps a few gold medals as well … and like the Olympics, without the close attention of the media the public would know very little of it.

Scarcely a day goes by when there is no new discovery of fraud or theft committed by individuals, groups, or companies. Our newspapers are replete with announcements of one sordid deal after another. Often the culprits are officials in local or provincial government. But corruption is not limited to those at a lower level. In 2005, 40 members of parliament were charged with illegally using parliamentary travel vouchers for themselves, their families and friends. The sum involved in the Travelgate scandal was in excess of R10 million. However, it goes even higher up than ordinary parliamentarians. The arms deal is a classic example of this, with a president, a deputy president, ministers, deputy ministers and directors-general alleged to have been involved. When Jacob Zuma's friend, Schabir Shaik, was tried and found guilty of corruption, having solicited a R500 000-a-year bribe for Zuma from a French arms dealer, Judge Hilary Squires pronounced the evidence of his having a corrupt relationship with Zuma 'really overwhelming'. Zuma escaped being tried on charges of corruption, and then on expanded charges of racketeering, money laundering, fraud and corruption, by the skin of his teeth. The charges still hang over him as the DA struggles to have them reinstated.

One definition of corruption in South Africa could be the use of public resources, bribery, nepotism and political favouritism in order to secure absolute loyalty to the party. Another way of describing corruption is that it is blatant theft. The 2012 Transparency International corruption perception index ranked South Africa at 69 out of 176 countries. This means that we are better off than many countries, and it reminds us that South Africa is not alone in the corruption business, but it also tells us that there are 68 countries that have a better record than we do, so we have nothing to be proud of. We should never forget that companies implicated in arms deal-related charges come from all over the world, including Britain, France and Germany.

It could be argued that theft or fraud often begin with bribery, and the private sector is more often than not involved. The latest annual report of the Competition Commission reveals a long list of companies, both big and small, guilty of price fixing – from cartels deciding the price of basic commodities such as bread to construction companies colluding in contracts for the building of stadia for the 2010 soccer World Cup. Corruption in the private sector is serious and has a detrimental effect on consumers, and it seems that chief executives of those companies who are found guilty are seldom penalised. Regrettably, in almost every case they get off scot-free.

It seems therefore that wherever we look, in both the public and the private sectors, we see the ugly face of corruption. We even have a word for the one of its most glaring forms: 'tenderpreneurism'. From ex-ANC Youth League leader Julius Malema to the public service, there are countless examples of the fixing of prices in tender processes. This high level of corruption is very lucrative and therefore very popular. Despite the plethora of reports detailing incidents of corruption involving millions of rands, it is probable that what the public knows could be likened to the tip of the iceberg. Corruption has become so commonplace that few are surprised to read of the latest incidents of fraud. This is probably one of its most worrying features – that South Africans have almost come to expect and live with corruption as being endemic and inevitable.

Corruption in the public sector is more serious than any other, as it robs the state of resources which could be used for education, health and social upliftment. The most serious consequence of corruption in the public sector is that it hits the poorest of the poor. In the judgment quoted at the beginning of the chapter (*Hugh Glenister v the President of the Republic of South Africa*) the court held that:

> Corruption blatantly undermines the democratic ethos, the institutions of democracy, the rule of law and the foundational values of our nascent constitutional project. It fuels maladministration and public fraudulence and imperils the capacity of the state to fulfil its obligations to respect, protect, promote and fulfil all the rights enshrined in the bill of rights. When corruption and organised crime flourish, sustainable development and economic growth are stunted and in turn the stability and security of society is put at risk.

The same judgment also quoted the words of Kofi Annan, former secretary-general of the United Nations:

> This evil phenomenon is found in all countries, big and small, rich and poor, but it is in the developing world that its effects are most destructive. Corruption hurts the poor disproportionately by diverting funds intended for development, undermining a government's ability to provide basic services, feeding inequality and injustice and discouraging foreign investment and aid. Corruption is a key element in economic underperformance and a major obstacle to poverty alleviation and development. (*Ibid*)

It follows that the courts ought to be merciless; they need to be seen to be taking the toughest action against those who are found guilty of corruption. There ought to be zero tolerance when it comes to corrupt officials, no matter at what level they are found. However, it is not easy to successfully charge the culprits of corruption because corruption is also rife in the police force. We have lost two police commissioners very recently as a direct result of their fraudulent actions.

I recall when I was working at the Truth and Reconciliation Commission that I had two young policemen appointed as bodyguards and drivers. I got quite close to one of them. He was about 24 and we often talked about the post-apartheid developments and the work of the TRC. He was conservative but believed deeply in his responsibility as a bodyguard, even though he didn't always agree with everything that the TRC was doing. I asked him on more than one occasion about the allegations of corruption in the police force. His reply was devastating. He told me that amongst all his contemporaries in the police force, he didn't know one who hadn't taken a bribe to drop a case, to lose a witness, to destroy a docket. When I pressed him on whether he had been guilty of such misdemeanours, he replied, 'My work is protecting VIPs and I haven't had the opportunity to commit fraud and I hope that once I am back in more routine work I will be able to resist.'

Mondli Makhanya, former editor-in-chief, Avusa Media, recounts a similar situation: 'I have a friend that used to work in the training academy of the police and he would say that when they train these young people at the colleges, they come out very enthusiastic about being good cops. It takes six months to lose them when they start working, because the older guys tell them, basically, this is the way it is done and this is how you will do it so that has become the culture of our police service.'[2]

A comment by Pierre de Vos on *Glenister v President of the Republic of South Africa and Others* casts light on the government's disbanding of the highly successful Directorate of Special Operations, known as the Scorpions:

> Corruption is a human rights issue and the only way for a state effectively to combat corruption is through the creation of a truly independent unit that investigates corruption with a view successfully to prosecute all those who have engaged in corrupt activities. I would guess that for most South Africans this is a pretty obvious fact. Sadly, in the past some in the ANC government (and the majority of ANC delegates at Polokwane) have shown itself to be less than enthusiastic about the investigation and prosecution of alleged corruption involving party leaders or involving those closely aligned to the ANC through mutually beneficial financial arrangements and family and friendship ties.

> Hence, the Scorpions were abolished and a new unit – the

Hawks – were created to investigate 'priority crimes'. But yesterday in the judgment of *Glenister v President of the Republic of South Africa and Others* a majority of judges of the Constitutional Court (in a brave and brilliant judgment authored by Deputy Chief Justice Dikgang Moseneke and Justice Edwin Cameron), found that the Hawks were not sufficiently independent and that the state had therefore failed to fulfil its obligations to respect, protect, promote and fulfil the rights in the Bill of Rights as required by section 7(2) of the Constitution.[3]

* * *

In considering the causes of corruption, we need to be reminded that the corruption in the present ANC government was foreshadowed by the National Party when it was in power. Former *Sunday Times* editor Ken Owen reminds us that, 'Behind the racial ideology lay a naked greed which, combined with the centralisation of power, secrecy and short tribal lines of communication, generated pervasive and growing corruption. The procurement of food for the prisons department or medical supplies for hospitals or strategic stocks to beat sanctions, became the path to fortune for people who would now be called "tenderpreneurs".'[4] He continues, 'Close ties were forged with an array of international gangsters like Mark Rich, Marino Chiavelli, arms smugglers, oil dealers and convicted mafiosi, contributing to a culture of underhand dealing which was the mark of later years of NP rule.'

Ken Owen, in his irascible way, continues, 'Nobody objected when I described the National Party elite, accurately I thought, as having "their snouts in the trough and their backsides to the nation".' This sounds very similar to the criticism of the African National Congress. Owen is of the view that the ANC is 'no more corrupt and avaricious than the NP and one of the reasons is that a free press can expose more than the hobbled press of National Party rule, but the ANC's corruption is more crass, more ostentatious, more concerned with the trappings of wealth, the mansions, the limousines, the convoys, the outriders, the bodyguards, the baubles.' And I might add, the sushi on the bodies of half-naked women.

* * *

The media has always been locked in combat with the government. Under the National Party the SABC was His Master's Voice. Television service was delayed until 1974 because it might bring unwanted influence from abroad – that is, until the NP woke up to the propaganda value of this medium and used it assiduously to promote their racial policies with strong censorship. The ANC followed suit by slanting television (and radio) programmes in favour of their policies to the detriment of opposition voices.

Owen reminds us that 'in the 1960's John Vorster, an intimidating presence who had introduced detention without trial to suppress political activity by both the PAC and the ANC, set out to bully and intimidate the management of opposition newspapers into softening their opposition. On his orders, the celebrated editor of the *Rand Daily Mail* Laurence Gandar was fired.'[5]

Owen points out 'the remarkable similarities to the ways in which the NP and the ANC have reacted to public scorn as expressed particularly by cartoonists'. Both preferred to kill the messenger rather than take to heart the message.

South Africa is fortunate in having a free press. It is the media beyond all other agencies and organisations which has successfully published incidents of corruption without fear or favour. This doesn't make them very popular with the state and the ANC has often criticised the media as being biased against it. But facts speak for themselves; time and time again it is the media, particularly the print media, that has opened cans of worms which in many cases have led to action.

At the ANC's 52nd National Congress at Polokwane in 2007 a resolution was passed urging the creation of a 'media appeals tribunal'. This was referred to again in the 2010 ANC discussion document and a number of references have been made by Zuma and by the secretary-general of the ANC to the need to have such a tribunal because they believe that the media is not impartial and is biased in particular against President Zuma and the ANC executive. It would be a great tragedy if this came to pass, particularly bearing in mind that there is still a very real possibility that the Secrecy Bill could become law.

The *Mail & Guardian* reported in December 2012 that –

> ANC deputy president Kgalema Motlanthe met with the South African National Editors Forum in late 2010 and essentially gave the industry a chance to tighten up its own self-regulation mechanisms before the ANC stepped in. The proposal forced the print media in South Africa to do some thorough self-reflection, and in late 2012 the press council revealed a host of changes to its regulations, which moves from self-regulation to co-regulation with the public. The changes take effect in 2013 and seem to have staved off the ANC's proposal, which has largely been dropped from the party's agenda.

It appears that the only reason why such a controlling mechanism is envisaged is that the media's disclosures are often an embarrassment to the government. But South Africa is enormously fortunate in having courageous editors and journalists who are willing, at some risk, to investigate allegations of corruption and make them known to the general public. This is not to say that editors and journalists are perfect and do not make mistakes. But people can refute the claims that are made using the same public media, not only in print but also on television and radio.

Further, there has been a severe cutting back of staff and trained and experienced journalists are few and far between. Dr Iqbal Survé and a consortium have purchased South African Independent Newspapers from its Irish owners. The *Sunday Independent*, *The Star*, the *Pretoria News*, *Cape Times*, *Cape Argus*, *Mercury*, *Daily News* and others will be under its control.[6] The SACP has declared its support for the takeover and it is fair to speculate that the new group will be supportive of the interests of the ANC and its alliances: 'When I connect the dots, they say one thing to me – that this is a buyout that the ANC is pretty with,' said Professor Jane Duncan of Rhodes University's journalism school.[7]

Survé has stated many times that he has been a loyal cadre of the ANC; as a medical doctor he was one of Mandela's physicians. He has been very critical of the media in general and has stated that the media should contribute to 'nation building' and report 'the positive'.

Survé has been very active on Twitter and included the following: 'Africa's march to media freedom and democracy will not be stopped by self-appointed supremacists parading as liberals who have clear agenda.'[8]

When one takes into account Secretary-General Mantashe's statement on radio (on more than one occasion) that 'the print media is the official opposition, not the DA', then it is clear that the interests of the ANC are going to be served by the new owners. This will call for progressive editors and journalists to be even more vigilant and prepared to hold up a mirror to contemporary politics and the action and inaction of government – to print and be damned.

It is to be hoped that media disclosures will continue to embarrass the government – and, hopefully more so in the future, the private sector.

*   *   *

Criticism of the ANC in relation to corruption is severe. But we remember that under National Party rule, civil servants measured status by having 'a merc, a cycad and a heart bypass. In the Cape it was about wine farms, Afrikaans culture and a history of the tribe.'[9]

Two events that took place in August 2013 give an idea of the continued pervasiveness of corruption. The first concerns the Walter Sisulu University in the Eastern Cape: 'The Walter Sisulu University staff was paid a bonus of R48 million last year. This despite the university recording the lowest pass rate, the highest labour unrest, the worst financial situation and the lowest graduation rate of all South African academic institutions last year. Director-General of Higher Education Gwebinkundla Qonde indicated that the sum paid to staff was to settle all wage disputes. The university is under Administration and was indefinitely closed.'[10]

The situation at the university is a poisonous brew of maladministration, reckless striking and corruption. The very least Minister of Higher Education and Training Blade Nzimande can do is to change its name so as not to continue to dishonour one of South Africa's greatest struggle veterans. This evidence of corruption directly affects the careers of thousands of young students who will be forced to join the ranks of the unemployed. Even if the university is re-opened, nothing can repair the loss of trust between the administration, the staff members and the students. And no amount of effort can replace the time wasted while the university was in a state of utter chaos.

Even more grave is the damning report concerning the alleged involvement of the chair of the Independent Electoral Commission, Pansy Tlakula, in tenders relating to the IEC's lease agreement. This strikes at the heart of our still fragile democracy. We have rightly prided ourselves on several national, provincial and local government elections which were pronounced free and fair, both nationally and internationally. If the allegations are proved to be true, Ms Tlakula must resign or be suspended with immediate effect. We cannot afford even a hint of corruption in the IEC. Tlakula has vehemently denied the charges. But the saga continues as Bantu Holomisa, the leader of the United Democratic Movement, has now taken the matter to court.

What then are the causes of the widespread corruption which is eating away at the very foundations of South Africa? First, there is no doubt that many who were disadvantaged and deprived all their lives believe deeply that they are entitled to share in the riches of South Africa. There can be no quarrel with that desire, but unfortunately it is not limited to the entitlement of opportunity; it often appears to be an entitlement to taking what can be termed ill-gotten gains. This is particularly true of (but not limited to) local government.

A further cause of corruption, in the words of David Lewis, director of the civil society organisation Corruption Watch, is:

> … a weak, fragmented state administration. It is weak because in a very short period of time we had to extend the state from a state that served a tiny fraction of the population to a state that served a population 10 times larger than it had served before. The former state administration was centralised and absolute control was maintained from Pretoria. Every tender, however small or large, came from that central control. We now have a very much more decentralised and fragmented system

of government. There are apparently some 9 000 points at which procurement decisions are taken in the Eastern Cape and around these
fragmented systems interests have coalesced and developed. Not only
is this a fundamental cause of corruption but it makes it difficult to
combat corruption.[11]

In this decentralised system, many who have been appointed to govern provinces have access to huge budgets, which has never been part of their experience before. This, coupled with the ANC's deployment of loyal but often
inexperienced members of the party, invites not only maladministration but
often corruption – the opportunity to spread wealth amongst the family and
friends; to become part of an association of thieves driven from higher up,
as shown in Malema's involvement in the Limpopo provincial government.

A fascinating article by Mark Heywood, executive director of the
public-interest law centre Section27, describes how power has been trans-
ferred from parliament to criminal elites. 'Surely,' he writes, 'this is the
only way to understand the government's apparent impotence in the textbooks tender in Limpopo and other provinces; the apparent immunity
of John Block and his merry men in the Northern Cape; the thousand
municipalities that seem hostage to somebody other than the electorate;
the deliberate perversion of the notion of "innocent until proven guilty"
to allow tainted persons to hold lucrative office while the broken wheels of
justice inch forward.'[12]

The spread of corruption is not helped by the criminal justice system,
which is in many instances dysfunctional. There are of course good and
honest policemen and women, magistrates and prosecutors, but the overall
situation is that people can get away with corruption because the criminal
justice system itself is corrupt.

Corruption, as far as the ANC is concerned, has its roots in its life in
exile. During those 30 years, in desperate times many ANC members and
officials resorted to desperate measures. There was a commitment to a seizure of power and anything and everything was up for grabs to secure that
power, even consorting with criminals and engaging in criminal activities.
It would not be too much to suggest that a great deal of today's corruption
stems from the state of mind which existed in the exile period. The loss of

the moral compass has not happened in the last few years, it seems to have happened a long time ago.

One fundamental locus of corruption started very early on, possibly during the negotiations themselves. The key culprits are those in the private sector who, in order to protect themselves, offered opportunities to leading ANC members to get rich very quickly and very easily. I am referring now to black economic empowerment (BEE), which was not a government initiative, but was introduced by the private sector at the highest level. This attempt by the private sector to protect its own interests is reminiscent of the deal struck by Anglo American in the 1950s when reacting to threats by the National Party to nationalise the mines: in brief, Anglo gave General Mining Corporation to the only Afrikaner-owned mining company, Federale Mynbou, which would later become Gencor, thus effectively cementing relations between English and Afrikaans capital and the apartheid state.

This type of arrangement has meant that a number of senior leaders of the ANC, either in government or having left government, are rich beyond measure because they have received unbelievably generous offers from the private sector. Of course there is always a cost involved – and that cost is collusion with the private sector to maintain the present economic system. The ANC is at home in big business, as Eleanor Momberg relates:

> The ANC's assets through Chancellor House make it one of the richest political parties in the world. The company was allegedly started by former party Treasurer-General Mendi Msimang as a funding vehicle for maintaining the party's headquarters ... The creation of Chancellor House significantly boosted the ANC's coffers, with assets worth R1.7 bn in 2007 despite debts of around R100 m not long before. Opinion on where this money came from range from arms deal backspin-offs to minerals and energy tenderpreneurship – with redeployed cadres and party sympathisers in key state positions providing kickbacks to party coffers. [13]

That the ANC is set to benefit from the biggest contract ever awarded by Eskom – R20 billion for boilers for the new Medupi power station – through a company in which Chancellor House has a 25 per cent share has provoked widespread outrage.

* * *

We have established that corruption has reached unacceptable levels and that although it exists in every country in the world at different levels, this does not leave room for any complacency in South Africa, where corruption costs the economy about R30 billion a year. The critical question is, what do we do about it? It is one thing to acknowledge that corruption exists and that there are many causes, but it is much more difficult to discern how to tackle the problem in a meaningful way which will be effective and long-lasting.

It is estimated that there are about 35 state organisations whose responsibility it is to prevent corruption, but their rate of success appears to be very low indeed. In June 2013 Minister of Public Service and Administration Lindiwe Sisulu announced that the government was establishing a new anti-corruption bureau which could be up and running by the middle of 2013. According to the minister, the unit will have wide-ranging powers to clamp down on corruption in all spheres of government, working hand-in-hand with other law enforcement agencies. What is interesting and encouraging is that the bureau will facilitate the protection of whistle-blowers. It is too soon to judge how effective this bureau will be in identifying and reducing the levels of corruption, but already there have been critics of this latest initiative by government.

Judith February, writing in the *Cape Times*,[14] was of the view that yet another agency would not make any difference, and that the emphasis should be on political will rather than one more administrative approach. One of her criticisms was that if the bureau is to make any impact at all, its budget – a mere R17 million – is totally inadequate.

Paul Hoffman SC, director of the Institute for Accountability, was even sharper in his criticism, arguing that the introduction of yet another agency, this time a 'bureau', would not make a great deal of difference. 'Effective anti-corruption work is only carried out by units which have a sufficient degree of independence from political interference and outside influences,' he said.[15] Hoffman made the point that political interference features regularly in any attempt to halt wide-scale corruption. There ought to be security of tenure for officers in any anti-corruption entity because so often – and he referred to the fate of Vusi Pikoli, the former head of the National Prosecuting Authority who lost his job after instituting legal action against Police Commissioner Jackie Selebi and then Jacob Zuma himself – if one stands up against the executive, one risks suspension or indeed dismissal. Hoffman concluded, 'It is to be hoped that the pre-election posturing of the ministers will be seen for what it is – mere lip service to the fight against corruption, totally bereft of any political will to actually do what needs to be done.'

Bongani Mlangeni, director of communications for the ministry of Public Service and Administration, was quick to respond to the criticism, refusing to 'trade insults with Hoffman', as he put it.[16] The bureau will not replace other state organs tasked with fighting corruption such as the Hawks and SAPS, he wrote, but will be 'different from other anti-corruption agencies or institutions as it will not have criminal jurisdiction. It will investigate conduct within the public service by public servants and other parties who are allegedly involved in corrupt practices.' In addition, the bureau's work will not end when public servants are found guilty of corruption and are removed from the public service. 'It will also be gunning for those who are corrupting civil servants.' In other words, there are two sides to the problem: those who are corrupt, and those who are the agents of corruption, encouraging civil servants to break the law. Furthermore, civil servants and companies or individuals found guilty 'will be named and shamed, in addition to being blacklisted from participating in any government activities across the three spheres.' Finally, Mlangeni stated that the bureau 'will look at a number of categories related to misconduct allegations including abuse of power, bribery, fraud and embezzlement'.

The new bureau would do well to follow the example of Finance Minister Pravin Gordhan, who wasted no time in firing the South African Revenue Services commissioner, Oupa Magashula, for transgressing the SARS code of conduct.

We will have to wait and see who is right in judging the establishment of a new anti-corruption bureau. At the time of writing, nothing more had been heard of it. What is clear is that there is a general mistrust of government. Even when it announces what appears to be a concrete action to stem widespread corruption, whether it be in the public service or beyond, there is a cynical response because tragically the government has lost the trust of people who are deeply concerned about human rights and democracy and are committed to anti-corruption.

In the judgment I referred to earlier, the Constitutional Court is crystal clear in its view that the state should establish an independent anti-corruption unit to investigate allegations of corruption. And the emphasis here is on independent. So long as it is within the control and purview of a minister or of a government department or even the executive, people are not going to take it seriously. What is needed in South Africa is an anti-corruption institute or commission which is backed by the executive but totally independent, well resourced, investigative, focusing not only on identifying corruption but also introducing education so as to discourage and prevent corruption. Furthermore, it ought to be a national commission led by persons of the highest integrity together with experienced and courageous staff. Obviously there would have to be strong liaison with many other organisations which I have already referred to and should also link up with schools and colleges and faith-based organisations in order to maximise the effort of its anti-corruption work.

* * *

As the arms deal commenced, Jacob Zuma, then deputy president under Mbeki, was starting work on his Nkandla homestead. Funds for it were among the 'loans' received from Schabir Shaik. In the intervening years nearly R210 million has been spent on this compound, and we still don't know who has paid for the extensive housing and facilities there. It is said you are known by the friends you keep; certainly President Zuma has some very strange bedfellows, and the more recent influence of the Gupta family seems to continue without let or hindrance.

South Africa is fortunate in the office of the Public Protector. Thuli Madonsela has shown ability, determination and courage in responding positively to reports of corruption wherever it may occur. Inevitably this has resulted in attacks on her integrity by some within the ANC government. Recently it was reported that pressure was exerted on her to stop the investigation into the Nkandlagate scandal.[17] To her credit, she has resisted these demands and we await her report with interest, knowing that it will be unbiased. She tells it as she sees it.

The *Daily Maverick* reported the intervention of government's so-called 'security cluster' as publication of the report became imminent:

> The Nkandla scandal is escalating as a result of the Public Prosecutor,
> Thuli Madonsela's provisional report yet to be published. The ANC
> was furious and the cluster of security ministers railed against her in a
> public press conference and took to the court to stay the publishing of
> the report on the grounds that it may be a threat to national security.
> Madonsela defiantly gave the ministers 5 days in which to read her re-
> port. They in turn complained they needed more time but Madonsela
> has stood her ground and refused to extend the time limit and so the
> impasse continues. Pierre De Vos puts it well; 'National Security is a
> much abused term, often deployed by governments to prevent the pub-
> lication of information that would embarrass the government or its
> leaders. The attempt by the state to pre-censor the Public Protector's
> Report on the use of more than R200 million of public funds to im-
> prove the private home of president Jacob Zuma on "national secu-
> rity" grounds, is a clear and reprehensible case in point.'[18]

Unfortunately Madonsela's term of office is limited in terms of the Constitution, because we certainly need people of her calibre and integrity to hold this office. The office of Public Protector is relatively well resourced but there are so many cases being brought to her attention that she obviously needs even more resources, both in terms of finance and staff, but she is a bright light in a dark world of corruption.

So too the Auditor-General. This is an office instituted by the Constitution which has on many occasions announced the lack of adequate financial management in all the provinces. Unfortunately, outgoing Auditor-General Terence Nombembe seems to have had to do this on an annual basis, and government spenders continue to act with impunity with regard to the responsibility for budgets and expenditure, with over R30 billion spent irregularly in 2012–13, according to the A-G's report to parliament.

The Human Rights Commission is another arm which can and often does act against corruption in high places. There is a view that it could be more robust in its opposition to corruption, but the existence of such a commission is to be welcomed and it is hoped that it, together with other agencies, will continue the fight against corruption.

One would imagine that the criminal justice system would be in the forefront of combating corruption. That there are good people in the criminal justice system, striving to be responsible in their work, is not denied. However, the fact of the matter is that the National Prosecuting Agency and the Special Investigating Unit were without leaders for a number of months before Zuma made new appointments in September 2013, one day before the deadline set by the Council for the Advancement of the South African Constitution. If the government was taking corruption seriously, surely they would seek out and appoint the very best people to lead these two vital organisations!

Although the government has a significant majority in parliament, this is another place where corruption can be revealed and challenged. This is particularly true in that parliamentarians enjoy privilege so that an opposition member of parliament can draw attention to allegations of corruption without risk and the media can publish the statements and speeches made by parliamentarians in this regard. Obviously it is hardly likely that ANC members will raise the question of corruption by any of their own members or departments. More is the pity, because it would be so much more powerful if it came from ANC benches.

What has helped in some instances to do battle against corruption is the role of the whistle-blower. However, it is a very difficult and risky undertaking to become a whistle-blower. Even when anonymity is promised, somehow the whistle-blower is identified. That person who has the courage to expose public corruption within government and outside of government is at great risk. They risk, as it were, being sent to Coventry; they are at risk of being suspended or even dismissed; they are even, when the odds are high, at risk of injury or even death. Therefore it is of the utmost importance to ensure that whistle-blowers are given encouragement and maximum protection so that they will continue to reveal corruption wherever it takes place. We should not underestimate the stamina that it takes to be a whistle-blower. Very often, cases brought to court as a result of their action last for many months and hang over the whistle-blower as a very real burden. We ought not to expect there to be hundreds or even thousands of whistle-blowers, but wherever there is one person of integrity who is willing to stand up and tell the truth, it can only be of maximum gain to the South African society and a blow against corruption.

Finally, let me stress again that the elephant in the room is none other than the president. There is a cloud that hangs over Zuma and has done ever since he was first accused of fraud and corruption. If South Africa is to be serious about reducing the level of corruption and if government is to be taken seriously in this regard, then it means that we require a change of leadership. Zuma must go. Whether this is remotely possible in the minds of the leadership of the ANC is an unknown factor. But they were very swift to remove Mbeki, and when the ANC begins to appreciate that Zuma is an embarrassment, it may lead to them taking the very radical step of either asking him to stand down, or taking action to dismiss him as president. There can be no doubt that such an action will bring a huge sigh of relief to many concerned people within South Africa, and beyond our borders, but more especially it will mean that we start a new chapter – hopefully with a new leader who demonstrates integrity and commitment to a constitutional democracy and is fearless in his or her attack on corruption, wherever it is found.

CHAPTER SEVEN

The Role of Civil Society in a Failing State

To me, civil society is at the core of human nature. We human beings want to get together with others ... and act collectively to make our lives better. And when we face evils and injustice, we get together and fight for justice and peace.
— DESMOND M TUTU, ARCHBISHOP EMERITUS

Desmond Tutu has a remarkable ability to put profound thoughts into a few words, and his definition of 'civil society' is no exception. A more formal definition is found in the Policy Framework on Nonprofit Organisations Law:[1]

> Civil society organisations is the collective term used to describe all types of nonprofit organisations. Civil society commonly embraces a diversity of spaces, actors and institutional forms, varying in their degree of formality, autonomy and power. Civil societies are often populated by organisations such as registered charities, developmental non-governmental organisations, community groups, women's organisations, faith-based organisations, professional associations, trade unions, self-help groups, social movements, business associations, coalitions and advocacy groups.

This is a discussion document, already in its third draft, and there will obviously be several more drafts before it is tabled in parliament. It distinguishes between community-based organisations (CBOs) and non-governmental organisations (NGOs). CBOs are defined as 'nonprofit agencies created by communities to address local needs. They are governed by volunteer governing bodies and staffed by volunteers and/or paid personnel. Many

CBOs receive funding from a variety of sources including grants, dona-tions, fees and fundraising but *government is the primary source of funding for most agencies.*' An NGO is a 'private sector, voluntary (usually nonprofit and non-sectarian) organisation that contributes to or participates in coopera-tion projects, education, training or other humanitarian, progressive or watchdog activities. In the context of South Africa, these ordinarily are distinguished from the community-based organisations by virtue of their organisational nature and formalisation (NGOs are more formalised and well established as opposed to informal CBOs).'

It is clear that the term 'civil society' embraces a wide spectrum of or-ganisations and endeavour. Small and large organisations all over South Africa consisting of remarkable women and men work with orphans and HIV/Aids sufferers, feed hungry children, care for the sick, educate the young, and much, much more. These actions, some small, others large, are certainly part of civil society. Some organisations are independent, others in partnership with the state at local, provincial and national level. This wider definition should never be overlooked; they are a vital part of what keeps the fabric of our common society intact.

However, there is also a narrower definition, that of civil society or-ganisations which seek to influence government policy, which offer alter-natives, which resist and criticise undemocratic policies and laws. Policies which are hostile to a human rights culture and a democratic society are challenged by organisations both small and large. An example of the kind of organisation that has successfully taken on the state with some measure of success is the Treatment Action Campaign, under Zackie Achmat's persistent and courageous leadership, which forced the state to change its dangerous and wrong-headed policies on the treatment of HIV/Aids.

Another remarkable and young organisation, the Right2Know (R2K), brought together a coalition of organisations and individuals to oppose the Protection of State Information Bill. This campaign was launched in a side room of St George's Cathedral in Cape Town on 31 August 2010. Key players in the early stages of the campaign included Hennie van Vuuren, employed at the time by the Institute for Security Studies, Judith February, then employed by Idasa, Mark Weinberg and Dale McKinley (former chairman of the Gauteng Communist Party, from which he was expelled for his critical attitude!).

From small beginnings R2K soon grew into a coalition of well over 100 organisations which were concerned at the draconian measures of the Secrecy Bill. It was not confined to Cape Town, with branches in Johannesburg and Durban. Initial funding came from the Open Society Foundation, but most of those who supported the initiative were volunteers. In a very frank interview with Murray Hunter, the current organiser for the R2K, a number of interesting and even fascinating factors emerged.

Their slogan was to 'occupy every space available', that is, inside parliament: in the committees, sitting in the gallery wearing R2K T-shirts, one-on-one interviews with MPs from parties in parliament on both sides of the aisle. But they also resorted to the streets and whilst they practised decorum inside parliament, they were rowdy and vocal outside. Hunter explained that they found conservatives in both the ANC and the DA who were keen to safeguard the security of the state (he described them as 'old Nats'!). To my astonishment, he singled out Llewellyn Landers (a former member of PW Botha's cabinet) as an ANC MP who worked hard to reform the law from within; he made obnoxious statements about the R2K publicly and in parliamentary debates as a cover. I was incredulous, but Hunter was emphatic: 'Some of the key amendments that were welcomed by us came through Landers with additional support from Deputy President Motlanthe.' Hunter was definite that despite many improvements to the Secrecy Bill, President Zuma should not sign it into law but should refer it to the Constitutional Court. R2K has expert legal assistance from the Legal Resources Centre as well as from Adv Geoff Budlender, who is helping to draft court papers, so it seems inevitable that even if Zuma does sign the Secrecy Bill into law, it will eventually land up in the Constitutional Court.

The R2K's particular concern is that there is a lack of public domain defence over and above public interest defence in the bill. In its view there is insufficient protection for whistle-blowers. Further, there is no protection for the recipient of information which may be deemed classified. So on the one hand, the person who is in possession of that information and passes it on to someone else may be able to justify their action. But there is no protection for the recipient, who could be a journalist, a researcher, a member of the public or even a politician!

It is encouraging to note that R2K is no longer a single-issue campaign. The Secrecy Bill is only one leg; another is to assist civil society organisations and service delivery organisations, mostly in townships and informal settlements, who are struggling for access to information. They lack the knowledge and skills to secure that information, to carry out their activities in their own communities. A third leg is a focus on media freedom, media diversity, and hearings on media ownership. It is R2K's view that without the freedom of the media to report fully and freely, many of the attempts by civil society to achieve justice and transparency would come to nought. Finally, R2K will continue to encourage whistle-blowers in the current climate of corruption and secret deals, and to fight for their protection.

A final question I put to Murray Hunter related to a report on civil society post-Polokwane, by Steven Friedman and Eusebius McKaiser.[2] In this report, Friedman, a well-known and respected political scientist, states, 'A look at the current state of South African civil society suggests that it is vigorous, effective – and shallow.' He continues, 'Civil society is shallow in the sense that its roots are not deeply located within the poor majority. Most of the unemployed, casually employed and informally employed are not directly represented by civil society organisations. Different organisations are shallow to differing degrees but almost all are unable to claim adequate proximity to and organised participation by the poor.'

I asked Murray Hunter whether he felt this was a fair criticism of civil society in general and R2K in particular. He agreed that the majority of civil society organisations do not have adequate grassroots links. These civil society organisations are part of the public discourse, they are recognised, they have influence, they have funding, but they are not often in direct relationships with the very people they seek to defend. 'The truth is that it is enormously difficult to link up with grassroots organisations. The Group Areas Act is as effective today as it was when it was first introduced. There are huge gaps in living space and the poor are so desperately struggling, either to find a job or to retain their employment, that they have very little time and energy and resources to even work in any kind of structured civil society organisation.'

In my own view, Friedman and Hunter are right. There is no question that there are seldom direct links between well-resourced, organised civil society organisations and the very poor. This has always been the case. But I think it is perhaps unfair to criticise organisations that do not have these direct links. This should be aimed for, should be worked for, should be struggled for, but in my view there is a place for civil society organisations that have the necessary backing, skills and access to good education and re-sources to speak on behalf of those who are unable to speak for themselves. It is one thing to be arrogant and have no consultation and no contact, but it is another to try desperately to hear the pleas and the cries of the poor and to then try and do something about it, even if organisationally there is no continuing, direct link with the very people that they seek to assist. It is a dilemma, historical and present, but I think that organisations like R2K and many others have tried hard to incorporate organisations from the poorest areas to help them to frame their campaign. I think they would be the first to acknowledge that it is an almost insurmountable problem.

* * *

Corruption Watch, with David Lewis as its director, has only been around for about 15 months and has already received over 4 000 reports of cor-ruption, with requests that Corruption Watch take action wherever it can. Lewis is not satisfied with 4 000 reports; he hopes it will become 40 000 reports and 400 000 reports, and if his organisation can provide the plat-form to amplify these reports and focus on them, he believes it could have a very strong influence on leadership in both government and the private sector. He is particularly encouraged by the number of reports his organi-sation receives from public servants, 'people who are very fearful but who are ashamed that the institutions they work with are being associated with corruption'.

As far as the future of Corruption Watch is concerned, they want to encourage reporting – the greater the number of reports, the greater the transparency concerning corruption within the country. They also intend to follow up with a number of campaigns focused on areas which feature in the reports they have already received. It is interesting to note that many of the reports concern corruption in small towns, 'mostly about nepotism in appointments, and this is not the end of the corruption but the beginning of corruption. In addition, many are about corruption in public procurements,' says Lewis. The campaigns will focus on schools, where corruption and abuse are rife, but they will also expand to include small towns. Lewis concedes that his resources are minimal and that he needs more staff because of the enormity of the problem, but the fact that there is such an organisation is encouraging in the fight against corruption.

Cosatu leadership was responsible for the Corruption Watch initiative, and as a result the organisation is often called 'Cosatu's Corruption Watch'. The general secretary of Cosatu is on the board, but Lewis argues that he is there in his personal capacity and that there are also leaders from Business South Africa and the Anglican Church on the board. He strenuously denies that his organisation is subject to pressure from Cosatu; it seeks to act independently.

* * *

Among many other organisations which strive for justice, one is the Social Justice Coalition, which has highlighted the degrading conditions under which many thousands of people live. Their strategy has been to visit townships where there is inadequate housing, degrading conditions and stark poverty. A recent visit to Khayelitsha in the Western Cape was reported in newspapers, with photographs portraying the deplorable conditions under which many people still live. They also visited the Eastern Cape and went to a number of schools where they found inadequate classrooms, lack of facilities, lack of toilets, poor teaching, poor attendance and the like. These visits seek to remind both state and civil society that we have a very long way to go before we can truly describe our country as one in which all people are adequately catered for.

While many civil society organisations are very unpopular with the government and the ANC, particularly those focusing on human rights and justice for all, it is true that civil society is not under the threat that it was during the apartheid period in our history. Fortunately the official policy of apartheid was expunged from the statute books and – at least until recently – it certainly looked as if South Africa was well on its way to a free, democratic society. Many in South Africa have woken up to the fact that power corrupts and there is a need for eternal vigilance.

We are certainly living in a more open society. We no longer read of civil society offices being broken into by security police; staff are not detained or imprisoned. This is largely due to our new Constitution and a Bill of Rights, and that is why we must safeguard that Constitution with every fibre of our being. Civil society was important under the apartheid state; it is equally important under a failing state. Everywhere we look, we see the dismal signs of that failing state in education, health, safety and security, the high rate of unemployment, the lack of housing and basic facilities for millions of people, the tragedy of Marikana, which saw 34 people being killed by the police, inefficiency, mismanagement, jobs for pals, and corruption in the public service and at every level of government.

* * *

Education or the lack thereof is another area crying out for major reform. Many educators and concerned organisations and individuals are not only commenting on the tragic situation which exists in many schools, but are urging the government at local and national level to accept that emergency measures and long-term planning are needed, particularly in primary and secondary schools.

In May 2013, a report entitled, 'The state of literacy teaching and learning in the foundation phase' was published by the National Education and Evaluation Unit. This independent institution paints a dismal picture:

> The majority of learners in poor schools start falling behind required literacy and numeracy levels in their first year, and by the time they end the 'foundation phase' in grade 3, many have effectively dropped out

and will predictably fail to master the curriculum in later years. This is the main reason why around 50% of children drop out of school before they reach matric. For example, last year's matric class started grade 1 in 2001 as a group of 1,150,637 learners but only 551,837 wrote the 2012 national senior certificate examinations.

A major reason for these unacceptable findings, in their view, is teachers who are not adequately trained to teach and/or do not have the commitment to do the job they are paid to do. They single out the negative influence of the South African Democratic Teachers Union (Sadtu) which is a strong affiliate of Cosatu and a vocal ally of the ANC. Tragically, because Zuma needs their support and their vote, he is unlikely to act against them.

Graeme Bloch has considerable experience in education and often writes very sensibly about the problem and the way forward. He makes the point that although our problems are enormous, we are in a much better place than we used to be. He notes that when he was a student, only about a quarter of students went beyond primary school. Now everyone does. The point he makes is that although things are very bad, there have been major advances in the field of education since 1994 and we should acknowledge and build on that. He suggests that we have three main problems: the first is the foundation phase, including maths, science and literacy; the second is the lack of high-level skills and equalities; thirdly, the focus on racial inequalities. 'All of these should set alarm bells ringing and red lights flashing.'[3]

Only about 35 per cent of young children in South Africa can truly read or count, Bloch points out. It is extraordinarily difficult to deal with high-level skills if the foundations are not right. He also points out that only about 50 per cent get to matric and even fewer to university. The answer, in his view, is not to rely on private schools; even if they grow as they are growing, they cater for only 10 per cent of our population. That still means that 90 per cent of our children are in the public system and it is there that our major focus ought to be.

Bloch acknowledges that private schools are part of the solution and that there is much to be learnt from schools that are professionally and well run, but that on their own they cannot be the solution, particularly as many of our children are poor and attend poorly functioning township schools. His third point is that all this takes on a racial dimension. 'While half of black children don't get to matric, 98% of whites pass. While maybe 15–20% of black matriculants go on to further study, some 60% of whites do.' Clearly we ought to be spending more of our time and resources where the majority of our children are, and that is mainly in poor and black populated areas.

Bloch is not entirely pessimistic. He agrees that we have to look at what works in other countries and learn from civil society in our own country as well as from those schools that are working, despite all the problems they face. He stresses the need for a national debate that would involve teachers and the government. 'We are right to criticise the government; it is their major responsibility to care for the educational needs of all our children, but we must find a way to work with the government, which has the money, the time and the officials. But we must not rely on them entirely. As employers, do the children of our domestic workers have food and light and books? Can we speak their language? Do we know their concerns? And people in the private sector, are we involved in the education of the children of our employees?'

There are no quick fixes, Bloch is quite clear; we are in for the long haul. But he, like so many others, passionately wants to see much more rapid progress which would give all South Africa's children a decent start in life.

A civil society organisation which has achieved a measure of success in the battle to improve the standard of education is Equal Education. An article in the *Cape Times* of 30 May 2013 describes how this fairly new organisation grew from very humble beginnings: 'It all started with 500 broken windows.' Equal Education's Yoliswa Dwane started working with the organisation in 2008, after completing her media and law degree at the University of Cape Town. 'We acknowledged no one knows how to change education systems, but we can learn from the experience of the Treatment Action Campaign, both from their mistakes and their successes.'

After a great deal of discussion it was decided that if there was going to be equal education, 'we had to fast-track our programme'. At a meeting in Khayelitsha, pupils were given disposable cameras and asked to take photographs of the problems in their schools. One such pupil, Zukiswa

Vuka, showed Ms Dwane and others a photograph which revealed that there were 500 broken windows at Luhlaza Secondary School. 'We decided that the Luhlaza campaign was the one we were going to take up. We spoke with the principal and the teachers and asked education MEC, Yusuf Gabru, for money to assist us in repairing the windows. This was a very small start but now we are moving with about 40 staff members and we have established relationships with a number of large international companies, which are funding our work.'

While the fixing of 500 windows was largely symbolic, it was a very important step and gave Equal Education the courage and determination to do much more. In November 2012, they successfully challenged and convinced Minister of Basic Education Angie Motshekga to agree to set minimum norms and standards for school infrastructure. Equal Education had been attempting to achieve this for more than two years and finally threatened to take the minister to the high court in Bisho. It was in response to this threat that the minister agreed to do what was required.

Commenting on this success, the *Cape Times* of 21 November 2012 outlined the very real weaknesses and gaps within the education system. 'Of the nearly 25 000 public schools in South Africa, 93% have no libraries, 95% have no science laboratories, 2 402 have no water supply, 46% still use pit latrine toilets and 913 have no toilet facilities at all.' Equal Education challenged the minister to use her power under the South African Schools Act to set norms and standards relating to classroom availability, electricity, water, sanitation, libraries, laboratories for maths, science and other subjects, sports facilities, internet, and security. Minister Motshekga has agreed to make available a draft set of norms. Obviously, Equal Education is not asleep on the job and will constantly remind the minister of the promise that she has made. Equal Education has a firm base in strong research and an emphasis on advocacy, community organising, setting of targets, demonstrations, and when everything else failed, resorted to litigation. This is a model for other civil society organisations to follow.

* * *

Despite successes by some major civil society organisations, all is not well within civil society as a whole. For example, in a recent briefing paper dated October 2012, the South African Catholic Bishops Conference parliamentary liaison office reported that until a few years ago, Idasa, the Black Sash, the Human Rights Commission, the South African Council of Churches and the Legal Resources Centre were all involved in parliamentary monitoring. Of these, the only one left was the Catholic Bishops Conference. This is a direct result of lack of resources, which has been a perennial problem for civil society organisations.

I recall, during the formation of Idasa in 1986, Van Zyl Slabbert and I tried very hard to secure funding internally, but to no avail. We were compelled to look beyond our borders and found significant and continuous support from Scandinavia, Europe and the United States. These countries were all opposed to apartheid and sought to assist institutions which were trying to develop a new democracy in South Africa. Very little has changed. The private sector in South Africa is nervous about civil society, unless it is a grassroots organisation assisting feeding schemes, education, clinics and the like. Those civil society organisations that focus on human rights, the development of democracy and the pursuit of justice find it extremely difficult to raise funds and are almost forced to look outside South Africa.

Until fairly recently there has been financial support from the international community, but with the economic downturn many countries have stopped assisting in this field. In particular, there are countries in Europe, Scandinavia and the United States which believe that since South Africa has been a democracy for nearly 20 years, it ought to be able to raise funds for civil society organisations within the country. This is understandable and would be much more desirable than dependence on foreign funding.

Furthermore, it seems that countries and foundations have adopted a new approach. It used to be possible for civil society organisations to draw up a proposal of action with a budget and ask foundations and governments to consider assistance. These days it seems that organisations outside South Africa want to dictate the agenda. They see from outside what they believe should happen and if they can find organisations that are ready to take on that responsibility, they are inclined to give support.

Some civil society organisations are fairly well resourced, but many have collapsed. A 2012 survey by Bridgit Evans of the Greater Good Foundation conducted amongst more than 600 NGOs shows that 44 per cent of civil society organisations report funding cuts of up to 50 per cent; 24 per cent report funding cuts up to 80 per cent; 11 per cent report funding cuts in excess of 80 per cent. Furthermore, 17.5 per cent report that they have no funding; 30 per cent have enough funding to cover one month's expenses; 35.8 per cent have enough funding to cover six months' operating expenses, and a lucky 16.7 per cent have more than six months' operating expenses. Idasa, a major civil society organisation with an outstanding record over more than 26 years, was liquidated in April 2013. It took about two minutes in court to bring to an end a quarter of a century of sterling work in the field of democracy, leaving a gap which will be almost impossible to fill. The reason for the closure: lack of funding.

Despite retrenchments and hard-to-come-by funding, the challenge to civil society has to be met. There can be no room for self-interest or self-serving; bearing in mind that CSOs have never been voted in to the work they are called to do: transparency, good management, sound financial controls, realisable goals and modest remuneration for office bearers should be the order of the day. Everything we demand of government must be reflected in the conduct of their business.

Both the state and CSOs recognise the need and the wisdom of cooperating wherever possible. The Constitution is clear: clause 59(1)(a), under the heading 'Public access to and involvement in the national assembly' reads as follows: 'The national assembly must facilitate public involvement in the legislative and other processes of the assembly and its committees.' Further, in clause 193(6) it states, 'The involvement of civil society in the recommendation process may be provided for as envisaged in clause 59(1)(a).' The recommendation process refers to the appointment of the Public Protector, the Auditor-General, the South African Human Rights Commission, the Commission for Gender Equality and the Electoral Commission. This is an extremely important provision, as it links civil society quite concretely with what is termed Chapter 9, which involves state institutions supporting constitutional democracy. It is to be hoped that both CSOs and the national assembly are aware of this possibility and will take steps to ensure that CSOs are involved in appointments of these critically important offices. The Nonprofit Organisation Act No 71 of 1997 makes explicit what is implicit in the Constitution: '... every organ of state must determine and coordinate the implementation of its policies and measures in a manner designated to promote, support and enhance the capacity of nonprofit organisations to perform their functions.'

As mentioned earlier, government at local, provincial and national level has very close links with thousands of CSOs and supports many of them financially. There are, however, a number of serious frustrations which exist in this relationship. Shelagh Gastrow, executive director of Inyathelo, the South African Institute for Advancement, has experience in civil society organisations way beyond her own organisation, which enjoys considerable success in assisting many CSOs in financial management and fund raising. In an interview with her on 21 May 2013, she referred to major difficulties facing CSOs in their relationship with the department of social development. Firstly, the Nonprofit Organisation (NPO) Directorate, which was established to ensure good working relationships with CSOs, is apparently understaffed and, as a consequence, highly inefficient. All CSOs are compelled to register with the directorate on an annual basis, but it is like a bottomless pit. The majority of CSOs send in their narrative and financial reports, but there is seldom an acknowledgement of receipt.

Recently, the directorate deregistered 30 per cent of CSOs, including Gastrow's organisation. She was in good company because well-established organisations, such as the Nelson Mandela Foundation and the Jacob Zuma Foundation suffered the same fate! There was an outcry so the department reregistered everyone and all CSOs were given six months to be compliant. To ensure that her organisation was compliant, Gastrow instructed her secretary to courier a copy of their report every week; no acknowledgement of receipt was ever received. Finally, after sending yet another email to the directorate, they received a positive reply. It seems that the intentions were good, but the new software being used let them down. As Gastrow put it, 'It is like putting a new engine into an old motorbike – when you take off, the whole bike blows up. It is so frustrating and time-wasting.' However, Gastrow told me that the new NPO bill referred to at the beginning of the chapter[4] will hopefully rectify these inefficiencies and provide a more realistic budget.

Neville Gabriel, the executive director of the Southern Africa Trust, appears to be a little more positive than Gastrow, stating that the department of social development 'seeks to simplify nonprofit organisations' registration procedures, strengthen relations with the NPO sector and improve its ability to manage the large number of registered NPOs, about 98 000 at last count.'[5] As an example of this good intention, he writes about the national summit with NPOs which the government organised in 2012, which was preceded by a series of provincial dialogues. He is ambivalent about the reasons behind this initiative by the government. On the one hand, it is clearly a pragmatic attempt to work with civil society groups which would enable government to be more successful in its delivery of essential services. But he continues, 'The government's drive towards a closer working relationship with formally structured non-governmental organisations is part of an effort to quell a rising tide of social discontent and protest about the stubborn levels of poverty and inequality linked to inefficient and corrupt state delivery arms.' He makes the point that this raises a dilemma for CSOs: on the one hand it is very important to have a good working relationship with the department of social development, but on the other hand they don't want to be used by government to cover up its own inadequacies.

A second major problem identified by Shelagh Gastrow is the administration of the National Lottery Distribution Trust Fund (NLDTF) and the National Development Agency (NDA). In a research report published in 2011,[6] Gastrow's institute, together with the Community Development Resource Association (CDRA), the Rural Education Access Programme (REAP) and the Social Change Assistance Trust (SCAT), outlined just how problematic the NLDTF and the NDA are. The report moves beyond anecdotal complaints to in-depth research, and the picture presented by its findings is gloomy. These worrying findings were drawn from a review of existing literature on the NLDTF, which included the board's annual reports from 2000 to 2009, minutes of parliamentary committee briefings, media reports and research reports that documented the grant-making activities of the NLDTF since 2000.

The structure of the NLDTF is complicated and often confusing, but simply put, funds in the NLDTF must be allocated and disbursed to non-profit projects in four categories: reconstruction and development (this ministry no longer exists and therefore no allocations have been made);[7] charities; sport and recreation; and arts, culture and national heritage. Applications for funds in these three categories are adjudicated by distributing agencies (DAs) appointed by the minister of trade and industry in consultation with the ministers responsible for these functions in the national government. In addition, the minister of trade and industry, in consultation with the minister of finance and the National Lottery Board (NLB), has the power to make grants from lottery funds earmarked for distribution in a fourth category, the 'miscellaneous' category.[8]

Certain key problems have emerged in respect of the disbursement of national lottery funds. According to the research report, the NLB's grant-making has been riddled with 'ineffective and sometimes confusing lines of communication and accountability between the NLB, the minister and the three DAs. The consequence has been that no-one associated with national lottery grant-making has been accountable for the NLB's inability to disburse funds effectively and efficiently to CSOs.' The report goes on to say that 'the minister has not been challenged on his decision to make grants from national lottery funds to state bodies such as the Commission for Gender Equality and the National Youth Development Agency.'[9] A further problem is the long wait between applications for funding and the reply from the NLB.

The NLB has disbursed less than 50 per cent of the available national lottery funds in each of the last three years. It is this gross inefficiency, lack of communication and lack of ability to spend existing funds that has caused many CSOs to either reduce their output or close down entirely. The good news is that the department of trade and industry is currently drafting amendments to the National Lotteries Act to improve grant-making. The recommendations offered by the research report include:

> Firstly, transforming the relationship between civil society organisations and state funding agencies towards more effective support to and strengthening of a vibrant civil society that plays an active role in

determining approaches to poverty alleviation. Secondly, positioning both state funding agencies as key to the development, nonprofit and funding sectors and recommending ways of developing more accountable and effective state agency/civil society partnerships. Thirdly, the need for civil society to organise itself more effectively to contribute to improve grant-making through the national lottery.[10]

It seems that it is the old story: many of the intentions of the government are worthy and good, but what causes the poor performance is the lack of communication, poor management, bad appointments, lack of transparency and unwillingness to recognise that government needs skills, particularly in the managerial sphere, and could call upon people who have such skills in a much wider context than the narrow party appointments. Once again, if one knows someone in the government, or is related to someone in the government, it is possible to secure a position even without the necessary skills. This is not to suggest for a moment that there aren't very good, reliable and faithful civil servants battling to do the jobs allocated to them. It is nothing short of a tragedy that good intentions, in particular in relationship to civil society organisations, are often frustrated by this incompetence, which seems to be at every level.

* * *

Friedman and McKaiser's post-Polokwane report makes some very useful comments regarding the role of civil society and the state.[11] First, 'CSOs need to guard against the possibility of missing strategic potential as a result of persistent pessimism.' It is understandable that there should be pessimism, particularly with the downturn in the economy worldwide, the economic problems facing South Africa and the lack of resources from foundations, the government and the private sector, but Friedman and McKaiser are right to stress that there still remain important possibilities for CSOs. 'Second, it is critical that CSOs improve their credibility by deepening their support base. This might prove an important catalyst for getting the government to take more seriously the representations of

CSOs.' This again is a valid point. The government often stigmatises the CSOs in the field of human rights and justice as a few hysterical voices critical of the ANC, which means that they are not hearing the deeper questions that are being put by CSOs. 'Third, CSOs need to find ways to achieve their goals in the broader political realm and in society beyond the formal political arena and not view direct access to government as the sole criterion for success.' Again, they are very much on the money. Civil society organisations need to reach out to a much wider audience and have a direct impact, particularly with business and trade unions, which form part of civil society – although Cosatu has ruled itself out of that definition through its close alliance with the ANC.

The report praises a lot of the work being done, but it comes back to the question of a weakness within civil society. Civil society organisations 'are overshadowed by strong evidence that civil society in South Africa is itself shallow because many people to do not enjoy access to it. This ensures that for all the inequalities within civil society, the most important divide between who is heard and who is ignored is not within civil society but between it and the rest of society in which many have the formal citizenship rights which allow them a say but not the means and contacts to use them.' Friedman and McKaiser continue to stress this point when they state, 'Civil society organisations which seek to address the concerns of the poor have not yet reached the representativeness which would enable them to reflect accurately the concerns and circumstances of the poor.'

These are extremely important points, but it has to be said that they are not new. For decades, certainly during the apartheid years, a number of strong civil society organisations which mounted vigorous attacks on the apartheid regime were often dismissed by many who were opposed to apartheid because they thought that these organisations were not transparent, were not consulting people on the ground, were not in touch with the vast majority of people living in townships and suffering the most from apartheid rule. It has a great deal to do with access to resources. If the leadership of a civil society organisation has access to education, to skills, to money, they can publish articles, gain access to the media, they can hold meetings, but those who are the poorest and most deprived, lacking these resources, are unable to mount their campaign of opposition in the same way as the more affluent organisations.

There is a rider to this, however: with the rise of the UDF and before them the Black Consciousness Movement, there was a very powerful attack on apartheid and vigorous opposition to the government, even to the point of making the country ungovernable. Perhaps there is room for both approaches – not so much making the country ungovernable but mounting protests in communities which are most deprived and also civil society organisations which do have access to resources denied to many. The big issue of course is communication. As already mentioned, the Group Areas Act no longer exists on the statute books, but it exists everywhere in reality. This means there is distance, there is separation, there is fear of people moving into areas where there may be hostility, even to those with the best of intentions. This is a real problem and will not be easily resolved.

A persistent question among many civil society leaders is whether or not there is a need for a new unifying body which could take cognisance of the 'shallowness' of some of the work of civil society and forge strong links at every possible level, including amongst the poorest of the poor. Some of these leaders, and they include many referred to earlier, such as Shelagh Gastrow and Neville Gabriel, look back with nostalgia at the United Democratic Front.

In his book, *The UDF*, Jeremy Seekings takes a look at the collapse of the United Democratic Front in 1991. He concludes that 'the UDF was dissolved not by design on the part of the top ANC or UDF leadership, but because of the breadth and depth of opposition and even hostility to the UDF leadership and the UDF as a coordinating body. Diverse groups within the broad Charterist movement saw the UDF as a vehicle of leaders whom they did not like and who they were pretty sure did not like them either, as a body which pursued strategies and tactics that they disapproved of and which controlled resources which should be re-allocated elsewhere. The final chapter in the history of the UDF is the story of an attempt to transform the Front to play new roles in new times, an attempt that was frustrated by the political forces unleashed under the umbrella of an unbanned ANC.'[12]

It may be that Seekings is being too generous towards the ANC leadership returning from exile and from prison. Looking back, it does seem that the ANC resented the influence of the UDF leadership and, in keeping with its approach in exile, sought to control every organisation, requiring them to be compliant with the ANC leadership.

Whatever the case may be, it would probably be unwise and misguided to try and revive the UDF. It has a cherished place in the history of the struggle against apartheid; many of its erstwhile leaders are now active in the ANC and/or in government itself. But there may be a place for some similar organisation to hold together the civil society movement, sharing available resources and skills and being in touch directly with those most affected by the continuing oppression of poverty and disadvantage. Whether this will ever happen is an open question. What is clear is that civil society has a very important role to play in emphasising the principles of democracy, transparency, integrity and justice in the context of a failing state.

CHAPTER EIGHT

Realignment and the Failing State

The ANC, while still politically dominant, is no longer unambiguously committed to the values of liberal constitutionalism. Its moral stature is at the same time much diminished by proven allegations of widespread corruption and maladministration. Most important of all, the ANC has failed to devise policies that show any realistic promise of lifting the majority of South Africans out of poverty.

— THEUNIS ROUX, *THE POLITICS OF PRINCIPLE*

In the preceding chapters we have seen how the ANC, with its lust for power, has sought to exert its control over parliament; it has threatened the Constitutional Court and tried to blunt the impact of a free press by the introduction of a Secrecy Bill. Its declared and passionate objective while in exile was the seizure of power and this remains its ultimate goal. With its focus on holding on to power and extending its grip on power, the ANC has failed to provide a vision for a just, peaceful and economically secure South Africa. Instead we have a ruling party with all the appearances of deep differences in its ranks, in an alliance which is at odds with itself, if not on the verge of splitting entirely, in the case of the union movement.

The difficulty of knowing who is really running the country creates an atmosphere of instability. Not only is there a lack of vision, there is also a deficit in leadership which threatens the peaceful and sustainable future of South Africa.

The ANC government has all the signs of a liberation movement which has not been able to transform its old habits into good governance. If we consider countries like Zimbabwe, Ghana, Sierra Leone, the DRC and Kenya, to mention only a few, it seems almost inevitable that a liberation movement finds it agonisingly difficult to shift from 'the struggle' to competent government, accepting the constraints placed on its control by the legislature, civil society, the judiciary and the media. The aim of the African majority in these countries was understandable – to throw off the yoke of imperialism and colonial rule. In this they succeeded. But it is one thing to oppose; it is another to govern successfully. All these countries and more made the painful discovery that liberation politics has to be transformed into a democracy and good government. Painful, because on the road to democracy they have experienced dictatorship, bloody violence, and breakdown of their economies. While instability is still present in many African countries, several have moved into a new democracy and continue to strive towards a sustainable peace. Ghana is a classic example of this transformation.

South Africa has thus far avoided becoming a dictatorship although it is a majoritarian government with little tolerance of opposition, and we have avoided violence on a massive scale, but as a failing state we need to be on our guard against becoming a failed state with all its attendant woes.

The cry from those who look with dismay on this powerful yet inefficient government is: what to do? It is not enough to bemoan the current state of affairs. Those who love justice and care about good government, the alleviation of poverty and the future of their children must move away from the armchair of criticism and do something!

There is no silver bullet; but a combination of a fearless judiciary, a viable and imaginative civil society, together with a consistent and wide-awake media, could make a substantial difference. As long as the ANC enjoys a large majority, this will not be enough to shift the logjam, however. The problem that has to be tackled is the ANC majority in parliament. This is where the laws are made (though policy unfortunately is formulated in Luthuli House), and despite the best attempts of the opposition parties, especially the Democratic Alliance, when the bells ring and the votes are counted the ANC wins every time. So the strategy must include eating away at the ANC majority – and this can only be achieved through the electoral process – unless the ANC implodes and loses its historical partnership with Cosatu and the SACP, which is not impossible, but improbable. The desire to hold on to power, the fear of losing that power, may well hold together the different factions and the alliance will probably muddle along. If the opposition is to offer an alternative then it must unite. But this will not be enough. There needs to be a realignment of political forces which offers a signal challenge to ANC dominance in the short term and an actual coalition to form a government in the long term.

* * *

As we approach the general election, which will probably take place in April or May 2014, there are a number of contending parties in parliament. However, the Democratic Alliance is the major player in the opposition stakes. In 2009 the DA secured 16.6 per cent of the vote, which gave it 67 seats in parliament. It has a powerful machine, strong financial resources, and has made inroads into black wards in local elections. It controls the Cape Town city council and the Western Cape province. Most importantly, it has Helen Zille, who is intelligent, courageous and innovative. She recognises that the challenge is formidable and has already sent strong signals that the 'white complexion' of the DA is no longer acceptable. The election of Lindiwe Mazibuko as the party's parliamentary leader sent a strong message to its own membership that blacks would play an ever-increasing role in its leadership.

Helen Zille is painfully aware that despite the electoral gains by her party, she has to reckon with the remarkably consistent level of support for the ANC – virtually unchanged since 1994. And this despite its poor performance. The lack of support for the DA in the Western Cape amongst black voters is a chilling reminder of the challenge which lies ahead. In 2009, the DA secured only about 1 per cent of votes cast in Khayelitsha and less than 2 per cent in Gugulethu and Langa. The party is desperate to increase its black support because it has virtually reached the limit of its support amongst minority groups and if it is to grow exponentially then it must attract black voters.

In my interview with Helen Zille in May 2013, she revealed her pragmatic approach to politics. Zille is the first to acknowledge that she relies heavily on her strong team. But she leads from the front and for many the

DA is Helen Zille. First, she analyses the different centres of power and when she sees a possibility of winning, she puts all her energies into securing victory. Her election as mayor of Cape Town against all odds is a case in point. Few thought she could win, but with political nous, verve and skilful strategy, she put together a coalition which secured the city council for the DA. In the same way, she saw an opportunity to wrest the Western Cape from the ANC and today she is premier of that province.

I was critical of her decision to leave parliament to become mayor, and I asked her if she would ever consider returning to parliament. Her reply was that if it seemed strategic and would be of benefit to her party, she would consider doing so. But I think she is glad not to be tied down in an arena which would give her little leverage and leave little time to be out and about in many parts of South Africa. I also think that as a highly intelligent person, she found the mediocrity in parliament very difficult to take.

I asked her about the DA's overtures to Dr Mamphela Ramphele. Zille told me that initially they offered Ramphele the leadership of the DA but that it was declined. They then offered to dissolve the DA and launch a new party with a new name under the leadership of Ramphele. This is an indication that Zille acknowledges that the DA needs black leadership at the very top, thus her readiness to give up her own leadership position. Whether it was legal to make such an astonishing offer is doubtful, but this is of no consequence because three days before the announcement was due to be made, Ramphele informed Zille that she was not going ahead but would rather form her own party. Zille told me that she was devastated and deeply discouraged because she had worked very hard for this realignment.

Clearly Plan A had failed – so what was Plan B, I asked. Zille replied, 'We will have to wait and see, but in the meantime the DA will go into battle mode and fight for every vote.' She was confident that they would increase their vote, because they had a strong team and were deeply committed to an open society with full equality for all. It was also clear that she hadn't given up on realignment and that Ramphele would figure prominently in the post-2014 election period.

No one can doubt Zille's courage and fortitude, but I got the sense that Ramphele's refusal was a huge blow and that Zille would like to opt out of her current position, possibly after the 2014 election. There is no question of her deserting her party, but I think her political activity comes at a high price, and she would probably want to put her considerable energy into a different field.

* * *

I interviewed Mamphela Ramphele in July 2013, after the launch of her party, Agang. I have known Ramphele for about 35 years and have deep respect and admiration for what she has accomplished in her professional life, despite banishment, harassment by the state and the murder of Steve Biko by the security forces. Nevertheless, I was surprised when she threw her hat into the political ring. So I asked her point blank, 'Why have you, a successful academic and administrator, manager of the World Bank, decided to enter the rough and tumble of party politics?' Her reply was straightforward: 'I have never been a member of a political party, I have never aspired to political office and I was enjoying looking towards an abundantly relaxing retirement.' But, she continued, 'despite my personal wishes, I had to confront the fact that our country is at a crossroads. If we continue on this trajectory, we will plunge into being a failed state. We have all the signs of failure, but we still have the window of opportunity and that window is provided by the firm foundations of our Constitution which are still in place. I want to do something before it is too late.'

This is a brave decision, because she has contributed so much already. She needs the tough challenge of party politics like she needs a hole in the head. But it is clear that she is so concerned about the parlous state in which the country finds itself that she is prepared to make the sacrifice.

Ramphele talked about her commitment to civic activism and recalled that towards the end of 2011 she had set up a Citizens' Movement which she thought would be the kind of approach which would halt the parlous situation that we were in. 'I realised though that this was not enough, it wasn't working, it had its limits. You have to have the power to change how we are governed and the only way to reach that is to contest the present government.'

I asked her why she didn't simply join the Democratic Alliance, knowing that they had offered her the leadership of that party, and had even gone further and offered to dissolve the DA, change the party's name and offer her the leadership. I put it to her that this would have made much more sense, because the DA was a going concern with a strong political party machine, which is necessary if you are going to take on the government. Her reply was that she wasn't looking for position, she wasn't a joiner, that there were moments of history in the DA with which she was not happy and she believed that there were people who would simply not vote for the DA even if there was a change of the name. 'What is missing in the DA is a transformational impulse in that machinery.'

Ramphele made the point that you didn't need a new name, you needed a new platform. I suggested that the task was formidable. She agreed, but pointed out that according to the figures she had, 41 per cent of eligible voters didn't vote in the last election. 'Secondly, there are many people who are now disillusioned with the ANC who are unlikely to be seen with the DA and thirdly, there are new voters, the "born free-ers", who come from homes and environments where they do not see any answers, so we need something new and that is why I decided that I would form a new party.'

Ramphele said that she had amazing support from young people, but it was clear that she was also aware of the harsh reality of trying to get people to commit. She was critical of the young professionals who are prepared to tell her that they are pleased that she is standing, that she has started a new party, but can't say so publicly because they may be in trouble with their employers or with the government. She added that she was also extremely disappointed in the response so far from older people, those who are 60 or 70 years old. 'They are the moneyed people, they are the people who have had the opportunities, they are the people who should be thanking God that there is one last chance for our country to really live up to its opportunity to be a great country, but they have lost their self-confidence, they don't think that the ANC can be challenged and therefore they sit back in their inertia and do nothing.'

Agang is very young and has had a rocky start, with no major names announcing that they will support her – in particular no key members of the ANC executive or leadership, despite possible disillusionment with the present government.

I pushed Ramphele to tell me what is going to happen after the shouting and the excitement of the election are over. She replied that Agang will do well enough to be able to go to the bargaining table and to form 'a coalition government'. Clearly, she has in mind the DA and other opposition parties, hoping that separately they can eat into the ANC majority and together they can overcome the massive support that the ANC enjoys. While I think Agang will do well to achieve even 1–2 per cent of the vote, Ramphele will bring strong cards to the negotiating table: she has integrity, she is intelligent, she is a woman and she is black. Strong cards indeed, which would almost guarantee her the leadership of a realigned opposition.

Of course, Ramphele has her detractors. There are many people who have commented on her entry into politics. There are those who admire her enormously, who are glad that she is taking this stand and will certainly vote for her. What percentage of the electorate will make that choice is difficult to say; it is early days. Others are critical and feel that Ramphele doesn't have the temperament for the tough business of fighting an election. Some have stated in newspaper articles and elsewhere that she is a very strong person, likes her own way, has had no experience of party politics and therefore the road is going to be extremely difficult. Politics is messy and conflictual. Ramphele does not suffer fools gladly, but she will have to change if she is to be a successful political party leader.

I was very surprised that in the course of our interview, Ramphele had some strong words to say about the media, particularly the print media. She is totally committed to the freedom of the press but feels that there is a mediocrity about much journalism in the country and very little depth in reporting, other than leading articles by various people from different groups and different ages which make reading the newspapers worthwhile. In her words, 'The media has not invested in professional development of its people and simply misses the point very often.' As a newly fledged political leader, she has learnt very quickly that without an alert and skilled media, the going gets very hard.

Another, quite different, actor who has come onto the scene is Julius

Malema. He has announced the formation of a new political party, the Economic Freedom Fighters (EFF). He is a populist, strongly in favour of nationalisation of the mines, the banks and key businesses, believes that there ought to be more equitable distribution of land for black people without any compensation for those living on that land, and is generally taking a very tough line against the ANC and for the poor. What has gone largely unnoticed is that two of his lieutenants came very close to winning local government elections in August 2013, standing as independents.

Despite his boorish behaviour, Malema should not be underestimated. He is pressing all the right buttons: land, jobs, poverty, white domination in the economy, and if he can persuade the unemployed and other impoverished people, he may be a force to be reckoned with. Malema appeared in court on 18 November 2013 on charges of fraud. Fortunately for him the case has been postponed and he will not have to appear before September 2014. This means that he will be available to participate in the 2014 election and could well take votes from the ANC.

*   *   *

Realignment does not mean merely the parliamentary opposition parties burying their differences and making a united stand. Even that is now impossible because of the various parties that will be contesting the 2014 election – when parties are in election mode, they work for themselves, which inevitably leads to fierce competition. It is almost certain that after the election, there will have to be a rethink and a genuine shift not merely to uniting opposition forces, but to a realignment. However, if that is to make any significant change, it will have to include a sizeable chunk of those who have in the past been consistent in their support of the ANC.

In the run-up to the election, the pressures on the ANC as the governing party may become so great that the cracks will begin to widen; there may be a shift in allegiance by their supporters to one opposition party or another. We should not imagine that it could be only to the DA or Agang; it may also be to the EFF.

One possible approach by all opposition parties, even prior to any future amalgamation, would be transparency in relation to funding. Ramphele has made a good start by declaring her personal wealth, which is not insignificant. It would be good for all political party leaders to do likewise. But as I wrote to the *Cape Times* and to *The Times* on 23 August 2013, she would in any case have had to declare her personal finances when she got to parliament. However, if she were to reveal the support that she is getting for Agang, particularly in large amounts, she would really set the cat among the pigeons, because the ANC, the DA and smaller parties have refused to disclose this information. I hope this will lead to greater transparency in the 2014 election. To that end, I think all parties should be challenged to come clean and to tell voters who their major financial backers are, so voters can gauge the extent of the influence of these backers.

This united stand would put huge pressure on the ANC to disclose their key financial backers. There has always been considerable suspicion surrounding those who contribute to the ANC, both from inside the country and from beyond our shores. There is very little doubt that big business will be supporting the ANC, as it will probably also support the DA and perhaps Agang. But the aim is for transparency in terms of those who give large amounts to political parties. A joint approach by all opposition parties, even before realignment, as I have suggested, would be a major step towards transparency and a huge challenge to the ANC.

Ramphele has given the lead; Zille must follow as soon as possible. Idasa strove valiantly to bring this about, but without success. Raenette Taljaard tells of her keen disappointment that her party, the DA, refused to disclose its list of major contributors. She writes, 'The party of principle which I had joined had taken, in my view, an untenable stance against full and unreserved disclosure of private funding, despite clear indications that such funding increases the chances of corruption and policy capture by special interests at all levels of government.'[1]

* * *

It is probably too early to forecast the percentage vote for each party in the general election scheduled for 2014. After all, a week is a long time in politics. However, it seems that speculation is rife: commentators are prophesying who will win, who will lose, and by how much. So let me add my thoughts to their number (I write this in November 2013).

The seasoned and highly experienced columnist and former editor, Allister Sparks, believes that the ANC is 'becoming beatable'.[2] He argues that on the basis of local elections held in July 2013, the ANC is losing support. He seems to have overlooked the fact that the ANC won 15 of the 20 seats contested. Yes, the DA won Oudtshoorn, but the ANC won Plettenberg Bay, despite its appalling record of non-delivery when it was in control of the Western Cape.

There are many similar prognostications sounding the death knell for the ANC. While it is understandable that those who oppose the ANC will want to cling to the hope that that party is a declining force, they seem to have overlooked two important factors. First, the ANC, judging by its history, will do anything to retain power and will use all its resources to maintain control. If one looks at the period in exile, one sees the ruthlessness of the leadership of the ANC in asserting rigid control over the party. There is nothing that suggests for a moment that it will take any threat from the outside lying down. 'Seizure of power' is still the watchword. Secondly, when the chips are down, the ANC is essentially a family rather than a political party. The response to attacks from outside the family will inevitably lead it to rally around, close ranks and support the ANC. Its history, its struggle, its songs, its heroes, its poetry, will all count. Further, black distrust of the white minority will almost certainly drive them back into the arms of the ANC.

We would be foolish to indulge in wishful thinking. The answer is to fight like hell and hope that eventually the strains within the ANC family will create fractures and fissures, enough to lead to desertion and a search for a new political home. Those in opposition should be ready for this, offering genuine, workable options rather than constantly beating the anti-ANC drum. This rhetoric, which helps to keep the opposition together, will only delay the fundamental change so many of us are anticipating. It will come, but not in 2014. So much will depend not only on the ANC and its followers, but also on the realignment of the opposition when they set aside their differences and unite to tackle a formidable opponent.

To back up what I am arguing, it is important to look at the percentages gained by the various parties in 2009. The ANC mustered 65.9 per cent of the votes cast, the DA 16.6 per cent, Cope 7.42 per cent, and the IFP 4.55 per cent. Other small parties had minimal support. So what can the major opposition parties hope to attain in 2014? There would have to be a major swing for the DA to obtain the 25 per cent which sources within the party suggest is their aim. It is more probable that they will gain 20 per cent, which would represent remarkable growth, but it is difficult to see them achieving more than that. The IFP will probably get around 3 per cent and Cope will show a radical decline to 1.5 per cent if they are lucky.

The two parties whose support is difficult to gauge, simply because they are so new on the political scene, are the EFF and Agang. I wouldn't be surprised if the EFF gained 5 per cent of the vote, which would see Malema and several of his stalwarts in parliament. This should provide fireworks and quite a lot of fun, but it also should be taken seriously. The recent demonstrations by the EFF have been ugly and menacing. More disturbing are the large posters which read 'Honeymoon is over for white people in South Africa', clearly racist in tone. Much more worrying is the placard which reads 'A Revolutionary must become a cold killing machine motivated by pure hate'. These posters are not handwritten on a small sheet of paper; they are professionally printed and must therefore have the approval of Malema and his lieutenants.

If this is the chilling tone in November we can expect a rough and ugly lead up to the election in 2014.

I think Agang is equally difficult to gauge in terms of its support. Since the launch, the party has hardly been visible and, on the surface at any rate, there doesn't seem to be a huge rush to join Ramphele in her attempts to attract a large body of voters. It may reach 1–2 per cent of the total votes cast. If we do the numbers, then it is difficult to see the ANC dropping below 60 per cent. From almost 66 per cent to 60 per cent is a significant drop, but there are those inside the ANC with whom I have talked, and other commentators, who think that it may well achieve 62 per cent.

While the figures quoted above are not a thumb-suck, there are many imponderables and many different situations will arise before election day

2014: the strife within Cosatu, one of the ANC's major partners; the constant friction and dangerous divisions in the mining industry; the clear friction within the ANC itself, all point to it possibly losing more support than I have suggested. But a great deal will also depend on the strategy of the DA. What it is discovering is that it is tougher to be in government than in opposition. In the Western Cape, for example, while both the premier and the mayor of Cape Town are upfront and doing sterling work, there are growing criticisms of the DA government in the province. It may be that this is a plot by the ANC to make the province ungovernable, but there have been a number of strategic mistakes made by the party leadership. It is extraordinary that the city council and the province cannot come up with a blueprint that will supply adequate and decent toilet facilities for the thousands who have totally inadequate facilities. There is the question of extending the city into Philippi, another sore point for many people. There is the fact that every single year people on the Cape Flats and in informal settlements are washed out by the winter rains and the only solution appears to be to give out blankets and food parcels, which of course doesn't solve the problem at all. The disturbances in the fruit industry in 2013 also point to a lack of strategic thinking and planning by, amongst others, the DA government.

The best thing the DA can do is to ensure that it keeps its election promises regarding the deprived and poverty-stricken areas in the Western Cape and shows South Africa that it can run a province, it can run a city, far better than anyone else. The odds are huge and the constant inflow of people from other provinces doesn't make the task any easier. Housing is still a very sore point for many who live in shacks. All this is a tremendous challenge, but the better the DA does, the greater is the possibility in 2019 of a new coalition, brought together not so much by anti-ANC rhetoric, but by good, solid, caring work by a coalition of opposition forces. This coalition will have to embrace not only opposition parties large and small, but also many thousands within the ANC fold.

Conclusion

No political democracy can survive and flourish if the mass of our people remain in poverty, without land, without tangible prospects for a better life. Attacking poverty and deprivation must therefore be the first priority of a democratic government.

— RECONSTRUCTION AND DEVELOPMENT PROGRAMME, 1994

This is a book I wish that I didn't have to write. But write it I must. It has to do with initial admiration, shared by many, of the ANC and then watching in dismay as the party started slipping towards a failing state.

Several years before the significant and far-reaching changes took place in 1990 I had met with a number of leading members of the ANC inside and outside South Africa. I was deeply impressed by the commitment and leadership of the United Democratic Front. They could not declare their support for the ANC openly for fear of prosecution. But is was crystal clear where their allegiance lay. People of the calibre of Cyril Ramaphosa, Jay Naidoo, Murphy Morobe, Trevor Manuel, Azar Cachalia, Sydney Mufamadi, Eric Molobi, Terror Lekota, Cheryl Carolus, Albertina Sisulu, Popo Molefe, Stone Sizani, the list is endless. They made huge sacrifices and many of them landed in prison.

I also met with many of the leaders of the ANC in Lusaka, London, New York, Sweden and Dakar in Senegal. They included Oliver Tambo, Thabo Mbeki, Chris Hani, Joe Slovo, Kader Asmal, Barbara Masekela, Albie Sachs, the late Steve Tshwete and many others. Because of my antipathy towards the National Party, the bearer of apartheid, I saw in the leadership of the ANC internally and externally a different breed of people and welcomed the difference. I concede I was naive and my expectations of what they could achieve were unrealistic, but I felt instinctively that they could only be a huge improvement on the apartheid government.

Of course meeting Nelson Mandela when he was released from prison and the frequent meetings Tutu and I had with him during the life of the TRC was enormously heart-warming and encouraging. Here was someone who stood apart, who could ensure that our journey towards a constitutional democracy could be realised. I voted for the ANC in 1994 and looked forward to a new era in South African politics.

After Mandela retired and Thabo Mbeki became president it was a different story. It is true that in those early years under Mandela and Mbeki the ANC's rule was highlighted by massive improvements and changes. For millions of people who walked miles to the nearest river to fetch water, the provision of clean water transformed their lives; the scrapping of the death penalty; the access to electricity for millions of people who had previously depended on oil lamps and candlelight; the de-segregation of schools, universities and colleges; the scrapping of segregation laws, all of this created a climate of reconciliation and new beginnings. It was a thrilling time and in the middle of all these changes was the TRC, which brought a measure of truth, some healing and closure to thousands of victims. After the dark and cruel days of apartheid it was good to be alive in South Africa.

But tragically the rot soon set in. The notorious arms deal, the wrongheaded and stupid policies towards HIV/Aids which caused the unnecessary deaths of thousands of sufferers, are some of the symptoms of an ANC which had begun to lose its way. The remoteness of Mbeki, his desire to control and his determination to show the world that Africans could govern despite the inexperience of the many people deployed into responsible positions meant that the honeymoon was definitely over.

Slowly I and so many others began to be disillusioned by the insistence on entitlement, the intolerance of opposition, the maladministration at every level of government, and the corruption, which assumed alarming proportions.

The situation has deteriorated even further since Jacob Zuma assumed office. A comment from an unusual source, the high-living Kenny Kunene, sums up the views of many regarding the president:

It's true, I like to spend, and I am not an angel, but unlike politicians I'm not spending tax payers' money. My real point is that, as a socialite and a businessman I meet many people, including politicians. When they speak to your face, Mr President, they tell you your imperial clothes are very stylish. When they talk to me, and feel safe from your army of spies, most of them admit that you, the emperor have no clothes.[1]

So, what went wrong? It forced me to look at the history of the ANC and in particular the ANC in exile. In preceding chapters I have shown that the oft-declared aim then was the seizure of power by all means. This should come as no surprise and I have deep sympathy for a party seeking power which had been powerless for so long. Think of what black South Africans endured through colonialism and racial policies for so long – fear, degradation, exclusion, separation from loved ones, imprisonment, loss of dignity, de-humanisation and even death.

But that was then and this is now. The legacy of apartheid still haunts us, but the ANC has been in power for nearly 20 years and it has failed in its original aim, 'Attacking poverty and deprivation must ... be the first priority of a democratic government.'

*   *   *

So what went wrong? The ANC in 1994 had its priorities absolutely right. But tragically it has departed from them in its lust for power.

In the first two chapters, the emphasis was on the slogan, 'seizure of power', which was the watchword of the ANC in exile. The question was raised whether this slogan has gone the way of all slogans and been left behind, or whether in fact there are those in the ANC, many of them in leadership, who still hold this as the ultimate aim of the party.

We have shown that words which characterise ANC governance and party policy include control, entitlement, party loyalty above all else, a belief that right is on their side. Despite extensive criticism stemming from many quarters, the party and its leaders are held to be above reproach;

however, at the party's heart is a commitment to unbridled power. There seems to be a pervasive fear of losing power, therefore grab all power.

Aung San Suu Kyi, the remarkable Burmese opposition leader who suffered house arrest and harassment for so long, said the following when she received the Nobel Peace Prize: 'It is not power that corrupts, but fear; fear of losing power corrupts those who wield it.' It certainly rings true for the ANC, which seems desperate to hold on to power and to extend its control in almost every direction.

Control is almost a fetish. It is not sufficient to control members of parliament; even mayors have to have their sanction, provincial premiers are elected by Luthuli House, all those who hold any office at all are under very tight supervision. The executive of the state has been replaced by the top six ANC leaders, who are Jacob Zuma, Cyril Ramaphosa, Baleka Mbete, Gwede Mantashe, Jessie Duarte and Zweli Mkhize. Nothing happens without rigid control and deployment to ensure that loyal cadres are in place.

The aim remains the exercise of power at every level, and leading up to the 2014 election, Zuma and other leaders of the ANC are calling for a two-thirds majority. To what end? To change the Constitution in order to increase the power of government.

A further question which was raised in an earlier chapter is whether the criminality and the culture of corruption which occurred during exile foreshadowed the criminality and corruption which is rife amongst ANC leaders and many in public service, and seems endemic in every government institution. Bureaucracy, maladministration, wrong choices, deployment, political incoherence, the high life enjoyed by the top leadership, were all in evidence during the exile.

If all of this could be seen as a passing phase, mistakes made by a new government, it would be disturbing but understandable. New leadership with integrity could appear and steer the ship of state into a more positive, more moral direction. But if it is symptomatic of the ANC over the last 50 years, then it engenders a deep sense of uneasiness, an ominous suggestion that a failing state could become a failed state if not checked. Very importantly, it also means that reform from within the ANC is impossible.

Of course, there are many good people within the party, both at leadership level and in the rank and file, and many of these faithful supporters of the ANC must be deeply embarrassed and even ashamed by the failure of the senior leadership. But because the culture of power seems to be so ingrained, genuine and extensive reform is simply out of the question. What is needed is a new coalition which will give South Africa a fresh start and enable it to return to the period which has been termed the Mandela years.

It is the ANC's obsession with power that engenders a culture of suspicion, distrust and extreme intolerance. This was evident in the period of exile and accounts today for the party's disenchantment with the Constitutional Court and much of the media, and its contempt for parliament. In exile, it could be argued that the ANC had good cause to be paranoid and lacking in transparency. After all, the movement seemed to be riddled with state security agents. But nearly 20 years later, the same phobias exist and the ANC is no longer an exile movement but the government of South Africa. The leadership has not yet learned the lesson that a besieged movement in exile is not the same as a democratically elected government. It remains obsessed with control and is more concerned with the state of the party than with good governance for all South Africans.

To develop this further, it means that even someone like Cyril Ramaphosa would not be able to turn things around should he become president in place of Zuma. He would certainly be a vast improvement and a more acceptable face of the ANC. He would push hard and strenuously for the implementation of the NDP. But the spirit of party loyalty at all costs, the lust for unbridled power, and the suspicions which run deep within the party are so deeply entrenched that he would be tilting at windmills.

I have great admiration for Ramaphosa and others like Trevor Manuel and Ahmed Kathrada, but they just don't seem to be part of the current ANC. They speak a different language and they would therefore have to be part of a new coalition with the injection of persons who are not ingrained Stalinists, who do not have a history of corruption or slavish intolerance or a commitment to the seizure of power by all means.

In my mind's eye, I see Ramaphosa and Manuel and many like them wincing at every new disclosure of fraud and corruption in the ranks of the party and/or government. I see them deeply embarrassed at the accusations and rumours of accusations concerning the president. It is difficult to comprehend how they and others like them have stayed and watched the decay set in. How do they live with a bumbling president, whose presidency is tarnished with Nkandlagate, inappropriate business associations such as that with the Gupta family, and the stench of fraud and corruption, allegations which will not go away?

Surely the time is long overdue for Ramaphosa and Manuel and many more good people within the ANC to declare that enough is enough; to lead a breakaway movement which could unite with other like-minded people currently in opposition to start a new movement to restore South Africa to a country that respects the rule of law and cares deeply enough for the impoverished millions to do something about their plight? They would argue that the ANC is their home and that they can do more to change things from within. Both have done sterling work for the ANC and the country, but already it seems that Manuel has been sidelined and there are mixed feelings about Ramaphosa and his dominant role in business. If they are not ready or willing to jump ship, then one can only hope that Zuma will be replaced by Ramaphosa.

Nevertheless the best scenario would be for a core of leaders from within the ANC and outside to focus on a new coalition. Where will these new leaders come from? I repeat that some will come from the ANC, possibly some from the labour movement, some from faith-based organisations, some from opposition parties and some from civil society. Someone who ought to be watched carefully is Bantu Holomisa, the leader of the very small United Democratic Movement. He was a general in the old Transkeian army and wielded enormous power as a very young man. He joined the ANC and was appointed as a deputy minister, but didn't last long in that position. He appeared before the Truth and Reconciliation Commission and during his evidence he accused Stella Sigcau, a cabinet member, of fraud and corruption. This was too much for President Mandela and he fired Holomisa on the spot.

I thought Holomisa was very brave and he remains a strong and articulate opponent of the ANC and a staunch supporter of human rights.

The word is that he still carries a great deal of weight in the Eastern Cape and there are many within the ANC who regard him highly. He certainly punches well above his weight. The coalition we seek needs new blood and people who have been on the periphery of politics.

The coalition will not come into meaningful power and significance tomorrow or even next year. But if there is sufficient will and deep concern it will happen. This is not mere whistling in the graveyard. Who would have thought that the once powerful National Party would in a brief few years end up on the rubbish heap of history?

Whatever the future brings, the battle is on, not only for the soul of the ANC but to ensure that a failing state does not become a failed state. This is where civil society, opposition parties, the judiciary, faith communities and the media will have to play a decisive role.

The ANC has dug itself into a huge hole, socially, morally and politically, and has taken South Africa with it. But we dare not succumb to despair and become paralysed in the face of the huge odds against our digging ourselves out of that hole.

In many ways we are a failing state, but we are not a failed state. Institutions such as the Constitutional Court and parliament are still in place. The media is largely free, civil society is still active. There have been other dark days (think back to the 1980s), and we survived and eventually triumphed.

I have no doubt there are sufficient good, capable and caring people in all walks of life who love South Africa and are prepared to fight against intolerance and the abuse of power to achieve a just society.

In the introduction I described the Mandela years as the honeymoon period in South Africa's transition to democracy. That ended when he stepped down as president after serving one term. But he remained visible, still active in offering his wisdom and insight. His voice and presence remained strong. In the last few years that voice has largely been silenced by illness and he left a void which was impossible to fill. On 5 December his voice was stilled forever, he died and our lodestar was no more.

But if the outpouring of grief and praise is to be more than mere words and gestures then all of us and our leaders in particular will have to give tangible expression to his vision for justice and peace.

145

In 2007 Mandela uttered these words which should be our challenge as we move towards the election in 2014:

> Massive poverty and obscene inequality are such terrible scourges of our times … they have to rank alongside slavery and apartheid.
>
> Overcoming poverty is not a gesture of charity, it is an act of justice. It is the protection of a fundamental human right – the right to dignity and a decent life.[2]

Notes

Introduction

1 *A Country Unmasked: Inside South Africa's Truth and Reconciliation Commission* (2000) and *A Life in Transition* (2008) dealt with my time as deputy chairperson of the TRC and afterwards as president of the International Centre for Transitional Justice.

2 A Boraine, *A Country Unmasked* (2000), p 321.

3 *Thabo Mbeki: The Dream Deferred*, pp 524–525.

Chapter One: The ANC in Exile: Early Years

1 Thomas Karis and Gail Gerhart, *From Protest to Challenge, vol 5, Nadir and Resurgence 1964–1979*, 1997, p 301.

2 Public statement, 'The Road to Freedom is Via the Cross', November 1952.

3 I Filatova and A Davidson, *The Hidden Thread*, p 202.

4 Matthews' speech was entitled, 'The Road from Nonviolence to Violence'. It is quoted in Thomas Karis and Gail Gerhart, *From Protest to Challenge, vol 5, Nadir and Resurgence 1964–1979*, 1997, pp 347–356.

5 'The politics of exile', *Third World Quarterly*, vol 9, no 1, January 1987.

6 Quoted by Blade Nzimande, Chris Hani Memorial Lecture, *Umsebenzi*, vol 10, no 8, 2011.

7 Janet Smith and Beauregard Tromp, *Hani: A Life Too Short*.

8 Karis and Gerhart, *From Protest to Challenge, vol 5: Nadir and Resurgence, 1964–79*, document 14, pp 388ff.

9 *Ibid.*

10 *Bua Komanisi*, 7 February 2008.

11 A Boraine, *A Life in Transition*, Zebra Press, 2008, pp 100–101.

12 Report of the Politico-Military Strategy Commission, 1979, document 114, quoted in Karis and Gerhart.

13 *Ibid*, p 724.

14 *Ibid.*

15 *Ibid*, p 729.

16 *Ibid.*

Chapter Two: A Government in Waiting: Exile in the 1980s

1 Security Council statement S/17413, 21 August 1985.
2 Gerhart and Glaser, *From Protest to Challenge, vol 6: Challenge and Victory, 1980–1990*, p 44.
3 *Ibid.*
4 *Sechaba*, 19 June 1979, p 11.
5 Stuart Commission, document 115, pp 539ff.
6 *Ibid.*
7 *Ibid.*
8 *Ibid.*
9 Truth and Reconciliation Commission Report, p 347.
10 Truth and Reconciliation Commission Report, para 43–47.
11 I am indebted to Mrs Jane Slabbert who gave me this letter.
12 Document 174, Declaration of the Organisation of African Unity ad hoc committee on southern Africa on the question of South Africa [the Harare Declaration], August 21, 1989 [abridged], in Gerhart and Glaser, *From Protest to Challenge, vol 6, Challenge and Victory, 1980–1999*.

Chapter Three: Parliament: Legislator or Lame Duck?

1 For a fuller account of Van Zyl Slabbert's and my resignation, see Boraine, *A Life in Transition*, pp 125–134.
2 Quoted from a paper prepared for the Norwegian Political Science Conference in January 2001 by Harold W Mathison and Elling Tjonneland.
3 Gareth van Onselen, SA Political Dictionary, http://inside-politics.org/2012/08/30/south-african-political-dictionary-cadre-employment-and-cadre-deployment/.
4 Raenette Taljaard, *Up in Arms*, p 57.
5 http://mg.co.za/article/2013-04-25-secrecy-bill-turok-wont-defy-anc-orders-this-time.

Chapter Four: People's Parliament

1 'Parliament of the Republic of South Africa: Task Team on Oversight and Accountability, Oversight and Accountability Model, South Africa, 27 January 2009', p 3.
2 *Sunday Times*, 5 May 2013.
3 *Sunday Times*, 5 May 2013.
4 *The Other Side of History*, pp 195–106.
5 *Ibid*, p 107.
6 *Ibid.*
7 *Ibid.*
8 ETT Report, p 18.
9 *Ibid*, p 31.
10 *Ibid*, p 31.

11 *Ibid*, p 67.

12 I*bid*, p 62.

13 *Ibid*, p 73.

14 *Cape Times*, 29 October 2012.

15 *Cape Times*, 29 October 2012.

CHAPTER FIVE: THE ROLE OF THE JUDICIARY IN A FAILING STATE

1 Max Sisulu, 'The evolving role of parliament in governance and accountability', in Daniel Plaatjies (ed), *Future inheritance: building state capacity in democratic South Africa.* The case referred to is *Speaker of the National Assembly vs De Lille and Another* 1999 (11) BCLR1339 (SCA).

2 *Ibid*; referring to *Mazibuko vs Sisulu MP, Speaker of the National Assembly, and Others.*

3 *Ibid.*

4 Sisulu, 'The evolving role of parliament in governance and accountability'.

5 M Plaut and P Holden, *Who Rules South Africa?*, p 163.

6 The first is *Soobramoney vs Minister of Health KwaZulu-Natal*. The second is *The Government of South Africa vs Grootboom* and the third is *Minister of Health vs Treatment Action Campaign*. He reminds us that in the Soobramoney case, the court found in favour of the state's policies 'while in both the Grootboom and TAC cases the courts determined the government's actions were unconstitutional'.

7 *City Press*, 14 January 2013

8 *City Press*, January 2013.

9 Judgment setting aside the interim interdict which has prevented the South African National Roads Agency from levying tolls on certain Gauteng freeways, September 2012.

CHAPTER SIX: CORRUPTION IN A FAILING STATE

1 Judgment: *Hugh Glenister v President of the Republic of South Africa and Others* [2011] ZACC6.

2 Mondli Makhanya's address was delivered at the Accountability and Corruption Conference in Cape Town on 26 April 2013 under the sponsorship of the Goedgedacht Forum of Social Reflection.

3 Pierre de Vos, http://constitutionallyspeaking.co.za/glenister-a-monumental-judgment-in-defence-of-the-poor/ 18-3-2011.

4 *Under the Baobab, Essays in Honour of Stuart Saunders on his Eightieth Birthday*, p 51.

5 *Ibid*, p 54.

6 *Sunday Times*, 9 June 2013.

7 *Sunday Times*, 9 June 2013.

8 *Ibid.*

9 This quote is from a book entitled *Under the Baobab*, a series of essays to honour Stuart Saunders on his eightieth birthday.

10 *Business Day*, 30 August 2013.

11 David Lewis speaking at the Accountability and Corruption Conference in Cape Town on 26 April 2013, organised by the Goedgedacht Forum of Social Reflection.

12 Mark Heywood, 'Coup by the connected and corrupt', *Mail & Guardian*, 31 August 2012. http://mg.co.za/article/2012-08-31-00-coup-by-the-connected-and-corrupt.

13 Eleanor Momberg, 'Chancellor House', *Amandla*, 13 September 2012. http://www.amandla.org.za/amandla-magazine/124-amandla-issue-2627/1595-chancellor-house-by-eleanor-momberg.

14 *Cape Times*, 19 June 2013

15 *Cape Times*, 25 June 2013.

16 Letter to the *Cape Times*, 1 July 2013.

17 *Sunday Times*, 8 September 2013.

18 *Daily Maverick*, 12 November 2013.

Chapter Seven: The Role of Civil Society in a Failing State

1 The Policy Framework on Nonprofit Organisations Law was published by the Department of Social Development on 31 July 2012. It outlines proposed amendments to the Nonprofit Organisations Act, No 71 of 1997.

2 Steven Friedman and Eusebius McKaiser, 'Civil society and the post-Polokwane South African state: assessing civil society's prospects of improved policy engagement', Centre for the Study of Democracy, Rhodes University/Johannesburg University, 2011.

3 *Cape Times*, 3 June 2013, from a speech he gave at a meeting in Stellenbosch, 1 June 2013.

4 At the time of writing the Policy Framework on Nonprofit Organisations Law is being circulated for comment.

5 Neville Gabriel, 'Accountability, cohesion and broken citizen-state relationships: framing the debate about civil society regulation in South Africa', Southern Africa Trust.

6 Stephen Heynes (compiler), *Meeting Their Mandates*, published by The Funding Practice Alliance in March 2011.

7 According to the Research Report this category no longer existed after the ministry came to an abrupt end. I assume that Reconstruction and Development now falls under the relevant ministries including the Ministry of Finance, Housing and Social Welfare and Development.

8 Heynes, *Meeting Their Mandates*.

9 *Ibid*, p 8.

10 *Ibid*, p 17.

11 Friedman and McKaiser, 'Civil society and the post-Polokwane South African state', p 7.

12 Jeremy Seekings, *The UDF*, p 18.

Chapter Eight: Realignment and the Failing State

1 *Up in Arms*, 2012, p 42.
2 *Cape Times*, 14 August 2013.

Conclusion

1 Kenny Kunene in an open letter to President Jacob Zuma, quoted in Pierre de Vos's blog on 24 June 2013.
2 Part of a speech at the unveiling of a statue of Nelson Mandela in Trafalgar Square in London.

Bibliography

Altbeker, Antony. *A Country at War with Itself.* Johannesburg and Cape Town: Jonathan Ball Publishers, 2007.

Amnesty International. *South Africa: Torture, Ill-treatment and Executions in African National Congress Camps.* Index number AFR53/27/92. London, 1992.

Asmal, Kader, and Hadland, Adrian. *Politics in my Blood: A Memoir.* Johannesburg: Jacana Media, 2011.

Booysen, Susan. *The African National Congress and the Regeneration of Political Power.* Johannesburg: Wits University Press, 2011.

Boraine, Alex. *A Country Unmasked: Inside South Africa's Truth and Reconciliation Commission.* Cape Town: Oxford University Press, 2000.

Boraine, Alex. *A Life in Transition.* Cape Town: Zebra Press, 2008.

Boraine, Alex, and Valentine, Sue (eds). *Transitional Justice and Human Security.* New York: International Center for Transitional Justice, 2005.

Butler, Anthony. *Cyril Ramaphosa,* revised and updated edition. Johannesburg: Jacana Media, 2011.

Calland, Richard. *Anatomy of South Africa.* Cape Town: Zebra Press, 2006.

Calland, Richard. *The Zuma Years.* Cape Town: Zebra Press, 2013.

Callinicos, Luli. *Oliver Tambo: Beyond the Engeli Mountains.* Cape Town: David Philip, 2004.

Chikane, Frank. *Eight Days in September.* Johannesburg: Picador Africa, 2012.

Clingman, Stephen. *Bram Fischer: Afrikaner Revolutionary.* Cape Town: David Philip, 1998.

Cronin, Jeremy. 'What Happened in Exile?' *Work in Progress* 81, 1992.

Ellis, Stephen. *External Mission: The ANC in Exile, 1960–1990.* Johannesburg and Cape Town: Jonathan Ball Publishers, 2012.

Ellis, Stephen. 'The ANC in Exile', *African Affairs,* vol 90 (360), 1991, pp 439–447.

Filatova, Irina and Apollon Davidson. *The Hidden Thread.* Johannesburg and Cape Town: Jonathan Ball Publishers, 2013.

Friedman, Steven and McKaiser, Eusebius. 'Civil society and the post-Polokwane South African state: assessing civil society's prospects of improved policy engagement', Centre for the Study of Democracy, Rhodes University/Johannesburg University, 2011.

Gerhart, Gail, and Glaser, Clive L. *From Protest to Challenge: A Documentary History of African Politics in South Africa, 1882-1990, Volume 6: Challenge and Victory, 1980–1990*. Bloomington: Indiana University Press, 2010.

Gevisser, Mark. *Thabo Mbeki: The Dream Deferred*. Johannesburg and Cape Town: Jonathan Ball Publishers, 2007.

Giliomee, Hermann. *The Afrikaners: Biography of a People*. Cape Town: Tafelberg, 2003.

Green, Pippa. *Choice, Not Fate: The Life and Times of Trevor Manuel*. Johannesburg: Penguin, 2008.

Harris, Peter. *In a Different Time: The Inside Story of the Delmas Four*. Cape Town: Struik, 2008.

Holden, Paul. *The Arms Deal in Your Pocket*. Johannesburg and Cape Town: Jonathan Ball Publishers, 2008.

Holden, Paul, and van Vuuren, Hennie. *The Devil in the Detail: How the Arms Deal Changed Everything*. Johannesburg and Cape Town: Jonathan Ball Publishers, 2011.

Jordan, Z Pallo (ed). *Oliver Tambo Remembered*. Johannesburg: Pan Macmillan, 2007.

Jordan, Z Pallo. 'The Crisis of Conscience in the SACP', *Transformation II*, 1990.

Karis, Thomas, and Gerhart, Gail. *From Protest to Challenge: A Documentary History of African Politics in South Africa, 1882-1990, Volume 5: Nadir and Resurgence, 1864–1979*. Pretoria: Unisa Press, 1997.

Kasrils, Ronnie. *Armed and Dangerous: My Undercover Struggle against Apartheid*. Johannesburg: Jacana Press, 2013.

Keane, John. *The Life and Death of Democracy*. New York: WW Norton & Company, 2009.

Lewin, Hugh. *Stones Against the Mirror: Friendship in the Time of the South African Struggle*. Cape Town: Umuzi, 2011.

Lodge, Tom. 'State of Exile: The African National Congress of South Africa, 1976–86', *Third World Quarterly*, Taylor and Francis Ltd, vol 9, no 1, 1987, pp 1–27.

MacMillan, Hugh. 'The African National Congress in Zambia: The Culture of Exile and the Changing Relationship with Home, 1964–1990', *Journal of

South African Studies, vol 35, issue 2, 2009.

Mandela, Nelson. *Long Walk to Freedom: The Autobiography of Nelson Mandela*. London: Abacus, 1995.

Mattes, Robert B. 'South Africa: Democracy Without the People?', *Journal of Democracy*, vol 13, no 1, 2002, pp 22–36.

Meli, Francis. *A History of the ANC: South Africa Belongs to Us*. Harare: Zimbabwe Publishing House, 1988.

Naidoo, Jay. *Fighting for Justice: A Lifetime of Political and Social Activism*. Johannesburg: Picador Africa, 2010.

Naidoo, Beverley. *Death of an Idealist: In Search of Neil Aggett*. Johannesburg and Cape Town: Jonathan Ball Publishers, 2012.

Ndebele, Nhlanhla, and Nieftagodien, Noor. 'The Morogoro Conference: A Moment of Self-Reflection', in South African Democracy Education Trust, *The Road to Democracy in South Africa, vol 1, 1960–1970*. Pretoria: Unisa Press, 2010.

National Development Plan 2030. Our Future – Make it Work. Department of the Presidency, South Africa.

Odendaal, André. *The Founders: The Origins of the ANC and the Struggle for Democracy in South Africa*. Johannesburg: Jacana Media, 2012.

O'Malley, Padraig. *Shades of Difference: Mac Maharaj and the Struggle for South Africa*. London: Viking, 2007.

Pauw, Jacques. *In the Heart of the Whore: The Story of Apartheid's Death Squads*. Johannesburg: Southern Book Publishers, 1991.

Plaut, Martin, and Holden, Paul. *Who Rules South Africa?* Johannesburg and Cape Town: Jonathan Ball Publishers, 2012.

Ramphele, Mamphela. *Laying Ghosts to Rest: Dilemmas of the Transformation in South Africa*. Cape Town: Tafelberg, 2008.

Ramphele, Mamphela. *Conversations with my Sons and Daughters*. Johannesburg: Penguin, 2013.

Report of the Electoral Task Team, 2003.

Roux, Theunis. *The Politics of Principle*. Cambridge: Cambridge University Press, 2013.

Salazar, Philippe-Joseph (ed). *Under the Baobab: Essays to Honour Stuart Saunders on his Eightieth Birthday*. AfricaRhetoric Publishing, 2011.

Sampson, Anthony. *Mandela: The Authorized Biography*. New York: Alfred A Knopf, 1999.

Seekings, Jeremy. *The UDF: A History of the United Democratic Front in South*

Africa, 1983–1991. Cape Town: David Philip, 2000.

Shubin, Vladimir. *ANC: A View from Moscow.* Johannesburg: Jacana Media, 2008.

Sisulu, Elinor. *Walter and Albertina Sisulu: In our Lifetime.* Cape Town: David Philip, 2002.

Sisulu, Max 'The evolving role of parliament in governance and accountability' in Daniel Plaatjies (ed), *Future inheritance: building state capacity in democratic South Africa.* Johannesburg: Jacana Media, 2013.

Slabbert, F van Zyl. *The Other Side of History.* Johannesburg and Cape Town: Jonathan Ball Publishers, 2006.

Slovo, Joe. *The Unfinished Autobiography of ANC Leader Joe Slovo.* Melbourne and New York: Ocean Press, 1997.

Smith, Janet and Tromp, Beauregard. *Hani: A Life Too Short.* Johannesburg and Cape Town: Jonathan Ball Publishers, 2009.

South African Democracy Education Trust. *The Road to Democracy in South Africa, vol 1, 1960–1970*, 2nd edition. Pretoria: Unisa, 2010.

South African Democracy Education Trust. *The Road to Democracy in South Africa, vol 3, International Solidarity*, part 1. Pretoria: Unisa, 2008.

South African Democracy Education Trust. *The Road to Democracy in South Africa, vol 4, 1980–1990*, part 1. Pretoria: Unisa, 2010.

South African Democracy Education Trust. *The Road to Democracy in South Africa, vol 4, 1980–1990*, part 2. Pretoria: Unisa, 2010.

Sparks, Allister. *Tomorrow is Another Country: The Inside Story of South Africa's Negotiated Revolution.* Johannesburg and Cape Town: Jonathan Ball, 1994.

Steinberg, Jonny. *Thin Blue: The Unwritten Rules of Policing South Africa.* Johannesburg and Cape Town: Jonathan Ball Publishers, 2008.

Suttner, Raymond. *Culture(s) of the African National Congress of South Africa: Imprint of Exile Experiences.* Free download from www.hsrcpress.co.za.

Suttner, Raymond. *The ANC Underground in South Africa: A Social and Historical Study.* Johannesburg: Jacana Media, 2008.

Taljaard, Raenette. *Up in Arms: Pursuing Accountability for the Arms Deal in Parliament.* Johannesburg: Jacana Media, 2012.

The Evolution of the African National Congress in Power: From Revolutionaries to Social Democrats? *Politikon: South African Journal of Political Studies*, vol 33, issue 2, 2006, pp 163–181.

Trewhela, Paul. *Inside Quatro: Uncovering the Exile History of the ANC and SWAPO.* Johannesburg: Jacana Media, 2009.

Truth and Reconciliation Commission of South Africa Report, vols 1–5, 1998.

Turok, Ben. *Nothing But the Truth: Behind the ANC's Struggle Politics*. Johannesburg and Cape Town: Jonathan Ball Publishers, 2003.

Villa-Vicencio, Charles, and Soko, Mills. *Conversations in Transition*. Cape Town: David Philip, 2012.

Waldmeir, Patti. *Anatomy of a Miracle: The End of Apartheid and the Birth of a New South Africa*. London: Viking, 1997.

Welsh, David. *The Rise and Fall of Apartheid*. Johannesburg and Cape Town: Jonathan Ball Publishers, 2009.

Wieder, Alan. *Ruth First and Joe Slovo in the War Against Apartheid*. Johannesburg: Jacana Media, 2013.

Acknowledgements

I would like to place on record my appreciation to Jonathan Ball who read the original proposal and agreed that it would be a book worth publishing. To Jonathan Ball Publishers and the team which encouraged and assisted me to bring this book to fruition. They include Ingeborg Pelser, Ceri Prenter, Jeremy Boraine and especially my editor Frances Perryer. I am grateful to Maxine Rubin and Claire Lester who, at the very outset, assisted me materially with research, which they did with considerable willingness and skill.

Geoff Budlender was the first person I talked to about writing this book and he encouraged me to pursue it. He also assisted me to receive funding from the Rausing Trust, for which I am greatly appreciative and I extend to them my warmest thanks.

As always, I owe a huge debt of thanks to Paddy Clark. She not only had to try and decipher my handwriting and my haphazard typing, but she went the second mile. She not only presented fair copy of every line that was written but also made many corrections and helpful suggestions. She is a person of great skill and has been of enormous assistance to me, and she is also a very special friend.

I would like to place on record my appreciation to the management of Constantia Place for providing me with office space which helped to facilitate the writing of this book.

I would like to thank all those who were willing to be interviewed. Their input helped me to formulate many of the questions and my attempts to give answers where there seemed none.

I want to place on record my thanks to former judge Laurie Ackermann for his very helpful comments on the chapter, The Role of the Judiciary in a Failing State.

There are so many people who have helped me including members of my erudite book club who unknowingly gave me clues and ideas when we discussed a range of books and enjoyed each other's company. To one and all I register my thanks – and of course all mistakes or shortcomings are mine alone.

Above all, my heartfelt thanks go to my wife, Jenny, who I imagine thought that I had slowed down and my research and writing had come to an end, only to discover that I was at it again. No complaints, lots of encouragement, and real steadfast care which was a constant source of encouragement to me throughout the writing of this book.

If this book in any way helps to focus on the dangers that South Africa faces at the present time and offers any proposals to try and avoid our collapsing into a failed state, then the effort will have been worthwhile.

January 2014

Index